Toward 1984

The Future of Appalachia

APPALACHIAN CONSORTIUM PRESS

BOONE, NORTH CAROLINA 28607

The Appalachian Consortium was a non-profit educational organization composed of institutions and agencies located in Southern Appalachia. From 1973 to 2004, its members published pioneering works in Appalachian studies documenting the history and cultural heritage of the region. The Appalachian Consortium Press was the first publisher devoted solely to the region and many of the works it published remain seminal in the field to this day.

With funding from the Andrew W. Mellon Foundation and the National Endowment for the Humanities through the Humanities Open Book Program, Appalachian State University has published new paperback and open access digital editions of works from the Appalachian Consortium Press. For more information visit:
http://www.collections.library.appstate.edu/appconsortiumbooks.

This work is licensed under a Creative Commons BY-NC-ND license. To view a copy of the license, visit:
http://creativecommons.org/licenses.

Original copyright © 1975 by the Appalachian Consortium Press.

ISBN (pbk.: alk. Paper): 978-1-4696-3674-0
ISBN (epub ebook): 978-1-4696-3675-7
ISBN (updf ebook): 978-1-4696-3676-4

Distributed by the University of North Carolina Press
www.uncpress.org

May 13-16, 1974

SOUTHERN APPALACHIAN REGIONAL CONFERENCE

Sponsored by
The Appalachian Consortium

Appalachian State University
Blue Ridge Parkway
East Tennessee State University
Ferrum College
First Tennessee-Virginia
Development District
Lees-McRae College
Mars Hill College
U.S. Forest Service
Warren Wilson College
Western Carolina University
Western North Carolina
Historical Association

ACKNOWLEDGMENTS Sources for Position Papers

American Petroleum Institute
1801 K Street, N. W.
Washington, D. C. 20006

Appalachian Regional Commission
1666 Connecticut Avenue, N. W.
Washington, D. C. 20235
Fed. Chairman: Donald W. Whitehead

Atomic Energy Commission
Washington, D. C. 20545

Chesapeake & Ohio
Terminal Tower
Cleveland, Ohio 44101

COALition Against Strip Mining
Washington, D. C. 20003

Commission on Religion in Appalachia
Ernest Nesuis, Chairman
West Virginia University
Morgantown, West Virginia

Common Cause
2100 M Street, N. W.
Washington, D. C. 20037

Duke Power
422 S. Church Street
Charlotte, N. C. 28201

E.T. & W.N.C.
132 Legion
Johnson City, Tennessee

Exxon Corporation
1251 Avenue of the Americas
New York, New York 10020

Mary D. Houska
Associate Professor, Economics
Hollins College, Virginia

Richard C. Jackson
Lees-McRae College
Banner Elk, North Carolina

Jack S. Kelley
USDA Forest Service
Box 2750
Asheville, N. C. 28802

LENOWISCO Planning District
  Commission
Duffield, Virginia 24244

Helen Lewis, Sociologist
Clinch Valley College
Wise, Virginia 24298

National Independent Coal
  Operators' Association
Post Office Box 354
Richlands, Virginia 24641
Louis Hunter, Exec. Secretary

Natural Resources Defence
  Council
36 West 44th Street
New York, New York 10036

Norfolk & Western
8 N. Jefferson Street
Roanoke, Virginia 24011

Pocahontas Land Corporation
Bluefield, West Virginia

F. Schmidt-Bleek
Environment Center
University of Tennessee
Knoxville, Tennessee

Dennis C. Shultz
Sierra Club
Matthews, North Carolina

Southern Coal Producers' Assn.
1307 Kanawha Valley Building
Charleston, West Virginia 25301
Quin Morton III, Exec. Vice Pres.

Tennessee Valley Authority
New Sprankle Building
Knoxville, Tennessee 37902
Chairman: Aubrey J. Wagner

United Mine Workers of America
900 15th Street, N. W.
Washington, D. C.

U. S. Steel Corporation
71 Broadway
New York, New York 10006

Cratis D. Williams
Appalachian State University
Boone, North Carolina 28608

World Future Society
Box 30369, Bethesda Branch
Washington, D. C. 20014

For further information contact:
Dr. Terry Epperson
Associate Director
Southern Appalachian Regional
  Conference
Appalachian State University
Boone, North Carolina 28608

TABLE OF CONTENTS

Acknowledgments	iv
Foreword	vi
Introduction	1
First Session: *Energy*	3
Second Session: *Land Use*	33
Third Session: *The Human Spirit*	71
Conclusion	99
Appendix A	108
Appendix B	113
Appendix C	128

FOREWORD

In the fall of 1973 a proposal was sent to the National Center for Improvement of Educational Systems (Department of Health, Education and Welfare, United States Office of Education) from Appalachian State University and the University's Task Force on Appalachian Consortium Affairs, requesting funds to support a conference on Southern Appalachia. The proposal was subsequently funded and the Appalachian Consortium was asked to co-sponsor the conference and publish the proceedings.

The funds from the National Center for Improvement of Educational Systems were administered through PROJECT OPEN, which was itself an outgrowth of the federal Training the Trainers of Teachers Program. Triple T was a $40 million effort by the United States Office of Education to get at the retraining of teacher trainers and break down the traditional walls that exist within educational systems and between educational institutions and their various constituencies.

The six cluster groups* in Triple T were deeply concerned with the organizations and systems that influenced educational institutions. PROJECT OPEN was a continuing attempt to move forward what had been learned through five years of Training the Trainers of Teachers experiences and to build on it. This past year, PROJECT OPEN activities have involved interactions among persons from public schools, universities, and communities. These meetings, held across the United States, provided a variety of forums and action opportunities for the development of communications that might contribute to new learning and improved community relationships.

The organization of the Southern Appalachian Regional Conference was built around the idea that local, insular change is an inadequate goal and that a dynamic social-change strategy could begin to build a connected movement of institutional and personal change that would go beyond the isolated successes and failures of individual programs and places. It was realized that this change process could not impose prescriptions and directives from above or from outside. No longer could funding sources concentrate on any one individual program or institution and thereby overlook the possible inter-relationship and inter-dependence of all of the parts of any social equation.

These conference proceedings will provide the reader with a classic example of how interested and concerned citizens in one region of our country got together to define common problems and propose solutions. It was known that these problems were being worked on constantly by various, discrete components--educational, political, economic, and social. It was hoped that the Appalachian Consortium with other organizations would be the constant mechanism for bringing together the coal miners, representatives of energy, zoning, and planning commissions, and those in political power within the states involved, to deal with each other and to listen to each other's point of view from some common base of information and shared concerns.

The plan was to make the group even richer by inviting those concerned with preserving and enriching the environment for the human spirit itself-- the preservation of our deeper value and the growth of personal learning.

Left to right: ASU Chancellor Herbert Wey, Governor James Holshouser (Conference Director) and Terry Epperson (Associate Conference Director) at the opening session.

When this combination takes place, the opportunities for new perspectives arise and new groups form and increase immensely.

The leadership of The Honorable James E. Holshouser, Jr., Governor of North Carolina, who directed the conference and Professor Terry Epperson of the University Faculty who ably assisted the Governor is gratefully acknowledged. Thanks also go to the Director of the Appalachian Consortium, Borden Mace. Special thanks go to Hazel Horn for editing the proceedings and to Kay Carfagna and Nancy West for typing the manuscript.

Herbert W. Wey
Chancellor

Appalachian State University
Boone, North Carolina

---

*Cluster Leaders:

Hobert Burns, California State University, San Jose
Richard Ford, Clark University
William Hazard, Northwestern University
Charles Ruch, University of Pittsburg
Eugene Slaughter, Southeastern State College, Oklahoma
Herbert Wey, Appalachian State University

Southern Appalachian Regional Conference
Toward 1984:
The Future of Appalachia?
Proceedings

INTRODUCTION

As part of Project Open of the United States Office of Education, the Appalachian Consortium sponsored the Southern Appalachian Regional Conference (May 13-16, 1974) at the Center for Continuing Education at Appalachian State University. To be sure that as many points of view as possible were presented, the Consortium solicited papers from diverse organizations. Those represented are listed in the acknowledgments.

At the opening banquet, the audience was addressed by Governor James E. Holshouser, Jr., North Carolina; John B. Howard, American Petroleum Institute; and Cratis Williams, Acting Vice Chancellor for Academic Affairs, Appalachian State University (Appendices A, B, C).

For convenience of discussion, the conference was divided into three main themes: Energy, Land Use, and The Human Spirit. The reader of these proceedings, however, will soon discover that these divisions could not be strictly maintained. Certain attitudes and conditions pervaded all three sessions.

1

Strip mining, for instance, was acknowledged to be a quick contribution to the nation's energy resources, but was condemned as a threat to the land and therefore to the spirit of the mountaineers. Deep mining, on the other hand, would require long-range development before adding to the energy supply, but would do far less damage to the environment and, by providing long-term employment, would contribute substantially to the well-being of the region's workers.

Another pervasive theme was how to retain for Appalachia its fair share of its vast wealth. Most of the profits now go to absentee landlords-- not just to the corporate mineowners, but also to the developers of the scenic areas and second-home resorts.

Other overlaps will become apparent to the reader as the films, position papers, discussions, comments, and summaries are covered in the following pages. The one general certainty seemed to be that each participant would go home, not only reinforced and better informed, but also aware of other experts' overlapping or discrete problems.

First Session: ENERGY

The session began with two films. The first, by Harley Jolly of Mars Hill College, showed the despoliation of Appalachia's mountains and streams. The junk yards and litter spots could be removed with reasonable ease, but other insults to the landscape appear to be ineradicable. The second film, by Phil Shelton of Clinch Valley College, showed efforts at reclamation--some good, some poor, some deliberate, some by chance-- but a dismal prospect over all. The films were only a prelude to the discussion of energy resources and their immense importance to the region--namely how to develop them with minimum residual damage.

An overshadowing problem is that, since the region does not control its own resources, the owning corporations can invest or not according to their own profit expectations and to the relative cost of other fuels. Too, the corporations are generally more interested in the current profit than in the long-term development and stability of the industry (although this may change when the international scope of the energy dilemma is fully realized).

Twenty small groups discussed various aspects of the energy problem--as it exists worldwide, not just in Appalachia. Summaries of the discussion have been distilled in the following paragraphs.

More than one speaker pointed out that the natives of Appalachia have lost control of the development of their coal resources because they are so independent they will not band together even to fight exploitation. They have divided themselves and can be conquered by any enterprising mining corporation (or land developer, for that matter). Laws cannot prevent an individual from selling his coal, land, or timber, but they should certainly discourage him from doing so, e.g., by regional zoning laws and state and federal long-range development plans. Above all, the local people, not the vested interests, should have the most say in the planning.

The use of Appalachia's energy resources should bring prosperity to the area, since it is expected to provide for the whole nation, but how to retain the profits is a complex problem. Small owners can lease their coal to large operators who, in turn, resell it at higher prices (and the strip scar may or may not be reclaimed). If deep mines are to be opened or reopened profitably, they will probably be so highly automated that they will give comparitively little local employment and, again, their earnings will go elsewhere.

Coal prices must remain competitive with other fuels, notably petroleum, by appropriate laws or other legislation. Improved technology such as liquefication and gasification at the mine-mouth might also help coal hold its price edge.

The short- and long-run effects of both strip and deep mining came up in many of the discussion groups. Stripping leaves the deep coal inaccessible and presents a reclamation problem. Deep mining removes the coal efficiently but requires expensive machinery and must follow costly health, safety, and pollution regulations. Cooperative and concentrated planning seems to be the only way to establish a workable trade-off between the advantages and the disadvantages.

If other fuel sources could be developed, high-grade Appalachian coal could be put to its best use, namely, in the metallurgical industries. Recycling waste and speeding the use of inexhaustible solar and nuclear power would go a long way toward solving this problem.

The Tennessee Valley Authority was both praised and condemned, for its ends and its means are frequently in conflict. It is pledged to supply cheap power, but to do so it often uses strip-mine coal, floods usable agricultural land, or commits other ecologically harmful acts.

Advertising by the public utilities was criticized by some as promoting overuse of a scarce resource. In rebuttal, it was maintained that such advertising sought to encourage conservation and proper use of water and power.

Many participants were concerned with the future of Appalachia and its dependence on coal. Fuel prices will undoubtedly go up, bringing profit to the region for some time to come but, in the meantime, the resources will be depleted. If other resources are developed, what of the coal? Are present legislators well enough informed to set up laws to protect the future of the area?

The speakers touched briefly on some points; they examined others repeatedly and at length. The principal concerns are apparent in the following position papers.

ENERGY

U.S. Atomic Energy Commission
Washington, D.C. 20545

OUR ENERGY PROBLEM. The Atomic Energy Commission believes citizens should know what they can do to assure abundant, clean energy in coming years. World reserves of fossil fuels cannot last forever, and before we run out, we must have good alternatives to take their place. We must also use the alternatives we have more wisely and efficiently.

Energy, of course, is essential to American life, but we are already experiencing shortages. Environment, technology, investment capital, foreign policy, trade balance, regulatory policies, and energy costs are a few of the complex factors that must be considered.

HOW CRITICAL IS THE PROBLEM? Our overall energy consumption is doubling every fifteen years, and our electrical energy consumption is growing at twice that rate. In the next 30 years we will need more energy than throughout our 200-year history.

We burn fossil fuel at the rate of 1.9 billion tons a year (accounting for more than 95% of our power) and oil at the rate of 18 million barrels a day. In less than 10 years, we will need from 20 to 25 million barrels a day.

The natural gas problem is more acute, even with foreign sources to supplement our needs for this efficient and clean fuel. In 1970, imports provided only 4% of our supply. By the year 2000, they will provide at least 28%.

Coal is plentiful (our known reserves are estimated at 2 trillion tons), but it is dirty--both to burn and to recover economically. Although strip mining is the most economically feasible method of obtaining coal, many ecologists want it completely banned.

WHAT ARE THE SOLUTIONS? As our energy will not remain cheap and inexhaustible, we must, for the short term, conserve it--if necessary by establishing priorities and rationing. For the longer term, we must reduce inefficient use and develop additional resources.

There is enough coal for hundreds of years, and processes are being developed to use it without contributing to environmental pollution. These include removing pollutants from coal during combustion or from waste gas before it goes out the stack and converting coal to gaseous and liquid fuels.

For generating electricity, nuclear power competes with fossil fuels, but it now supplies only about 1% of our needs; it will probably supply as much as 50% within 25 years. A high-priority nuclear program is the development of the fast-breeder reactor. This will extend the life of our uranium reserves for thousands of years, because it will use up to 75% of the uranium energy, compared with 2% by present-day reactors. These breeders are expected to be in commercial operation in the 1990s. Controlled nuclear fusion, by which the sun generates its energy, is also being developed. It would be safe and clean, and its probable fuel, deuterium, is abundantly available from seawater.

Vast deposits of oil shale promise increased oil supply. In the United States, such deposits contain more oil than the total world oil reserves. Costs for extracting the oil are not yet competitive, but improvements are being sought. In other areas, researchers are seeking ways to tap energy from the sun and to use geothermal energy.

Both in our homes and in industry, less energy can be used to serve the same needs through technological improvements and new standards for equipment and construction. Our ingenuity and resourcefulness are challenged to solve the energy problem by balancing conservation against the need for ample energy and a clean environment for future generations.

American Petroleum Institute
1801 K Street, N.W.
Washington, D.C. 20006

The United States is faced with a serious energy shortfall. It did not begin with the Arab oil embargo, but developed because oil was forced to bear a disproportionate share of our sharply increasing energy demands. Other energy sources were unable to furnish much additional fuel. Coal use was curtailed; nuclear power came onstream more slowly than anticipated; and little additional energy was available from hydropower. Inadequate development of domestic petroleum sources made it necessary to import increasing amounts of oil. Then came the Arab oil embargo--and we were faced with a crisis.

The crisis brought some benefits. The embargo reminded us that lack of energy leads to economic stagnation, unemployment, and spreading poverty, and that we cannot rely on insecure foreign supplies. If we are now convinced of the need to develop domestic energy resources, the embargo served us well.

The failure to develop domestic supplies was the result of many forces: the rising energy needs of a growing population, restrictions on energy development brought on by concern for the environment, fragmented policies and inappropriate government decisions that discouraged domestic development, lack of foresight by industry, and imprudent energy use by consumers.

There are three ways to solve the energy problem: decrease energy demand, increase energy supply, or combine the two.

Energy demand can be cut either by allocation and rationing of fuel, or by encouraging more frugal use of it. Allocation and rationing offer no real solution; they are designed merely to share scarcity. Conservation is another matter. Permanent solutions will take time, but most people can start practicing conservation today. Many Americans, however, still have no car, no air conditioner, and no TV set; they should not be condemned by energy scarcity to poverty or second-class citizenship.

Petroleum will have to furnish most of our energy needs for several decades. Coal, nuclear power, or new energy sources cannot supply enough to meet expected demand. Oil companies must go where there are large amounts of oil and gas, drill for them, move them to refineries--and construct more refineries. Six years ago, the largest oil field in this hemisphere was found in Alaska, but it will be 1977 before the pipeline is completed.

The Outer Continental Shelf alone may contain twice as much of both oil and gas as we have consumed throughout our history, but industry cannot drill without obtaining a lease. Until recently, lease sales were few. Offshore drilling must be accelerated to tap these resources.

Increased lease sales on the Outer Continental Shelf in the past year, the coming Alaska pipeline, and improved oil prices have finally brought an upturn in drilling after 15 years of almost steady decline. This will not bring an immediate increase in petroleum supplies, but is the surest route to increased domestic supplies and reduced dependence on foreign energy.

Duke Power Company
Charlotte, N.C. 28201

While the role of electricity has not been as prominent in Appalachia as in the more prosperous Piedmont Plateau of the Carolinas, it is beginning to catch up.

Over the last five years, for instance, in the 29 Appalachian counties of North Carolina, 112 new industries and 267 expansions of existing industries have resulted in $641 million in new investment and in a payroll addition of $127 million for 24,255 new jobs.

The six Appalachian counties of South Carolina, during that same period, acquired 81 new industries, 118 expansions of existing plants, and an investment of $706 million, resulting in a payroll of $92 million to be shared by 17,553 new jobs.

Every one of these 193 new industries and 385 expansions in Appalachia required electricity in varying amounts. When it was needed, it was there, most of it generated by Duke Power Company.

As for the future, the supply needed by new and expanded industry will be sufficient. By 1983, Duke Power will have expanded from a $3 billion investment to almost $12 billion.

Of the amount allocated for generation, $6.5 billion will be invested in nuclear generating plants with a capability of about 12 million kilowatts. Much of the remaining money will be invested in pumped storage hydroelectric power for peaking purposes.

Louis H. Hunter, Executive Vice President
National Independent Coal Operators' Association
Richlands, Virginia 24641

The United States, with 6% of the world's population, consumes approximately 33% of the world's total energy--much of it wastefully--and energy use has doubled in the past 20 years.

Of the energy we use today 50% is oil, 30% gas, 15% coal, 4% hydroelectric, and 1% nuclear. We have vast coal reserves in this country, much more than all the other energy sources combined. The Appalachian area should develop more mines, more safely, more economically, and with better reclamation methods.

The United States needs doubled coal production by the year 1983 from 600 million tons today to approximately 1.25 billion tons annually if we proceed with the present plans for coal gasification. We have been slow in this development and should strive toward it.

Coal is being gasified in South Africa successfully, profitably, and more cheaply than other sources of gas supply. The great amount of water needed for gasification is a real problem for our Western states, which have plenty of coal. This is one reason we in the Appalachian area should take full advantage of our surrounding resources.

Research should be done on a better method of heating with coal. It could be pulverized and cleaned and burned without a loss of even one BTU. It would be put in a completely sealed unit with very little waste going into the atmosphere. This can be done by recycling through water and other chemicals. Pulverized coal would be a great saving of other energy such as oil, natural gas, and bottled gas. Today there is a great loss of heat and energy through stacks and chimneys. Little has been done to improve the burning of coal.

Industry, with government help, should use the millions of cubic feet of methane gas being extracted from the coal seams and wasted by dilution into the atmosphere. Even small seams of coal (8- to 15-inch seams) could be burned in place and the different gases used instead of left lying in the earth.

The economy in Appalachia would suffer greatly if laws were passed to abolish or curtail surface mining. We must strive to keep good mining, both surface and underground, operating in our area. Surface mining is much safer and healthier than underground mining. Underground mines have been punished by much less production, because of many unneeded laws and regulations.

Tennessee Valley Authority
Knoxville, Tennessee 37902

Energy is so taken for granted in our society that only in times of shortage do we begin to comprehend its effects on our economy and on our daily lives. Energy supply has been vital to the advancement of civilization. To a considerable degree, man's wealth, health, and general well-being have directly reflected his use of energy.

For example, the average American citizen uses the energy equivalent of 7 tons--14,000 pounds--of coal each year and contributes $3,000 to the gross national product. In India, on the other hand, the average person commands the use of only 1/5 ton--400 pounds--of coal energy equivalent and contributes less than $100 to the gross national product.

One wonders how we let the present energy crisis arise. Besides population growth, the environmental awakening of the county has helped to precipitate the crisis. Our accumulation of environmental problems clearly could not continue, but in our efforts to reverse the trend quickly, we have created new problems. For example, to reduce polluting fumes from coal-burning plants, industries turned increasingly to oil and gas, our scarcest fuels, and this action hastened their depletion. Our concern that strip-mined lands be reclaimed has led to actions that in some instances threaten to stop the flow of coal from surface mines. Our concern for the discharge of heated water into our streams and lakes has delayed and, in some cases, stopped the construction of needed energy-producing plants. Another reason is the delay in bringing nuclear generating stations into operation.

There is a critical imbalance between our energy resources and how we use them. According to a recent study at Cornell University, only about 4% of our proven energy reserves is in oil, yet 42% of the energy we use comes from oil. Thirty-three % of the energy we use comes from natural gas, but less than 6% of our proven reserves is in gas. Coal, on the other hand, constitutes 86% of our known energy reserves, but only 18% of the energy we use comes from coal.

At the present time only 1% of our energy is supplied from nuclear resources, using what we call light-water nuclear reactors. If we rely solely on them, they can use less than 1% of the uranium ore we mine. This fraction constitutes just over 4% of our total energy reserves and would be exhausted in 20 to 30 years. However, TVA has joined with others to build a demonstration breeder reactor near Oak Ridge, Tennessee. If it is successful, it will produce from the balance of the uranium ore more fuel than it consumes and so extend the life of our uranium reserves to provide for our energy needs for many centuries. Obviously, to solve our energy problems, we must rely more heavily on coal and on the breeder reactor.

In the short term, heavy emphasis must be placed on conserving energy--turning down our thermostats, driving our automobiles less, and taking many other conservation measures.

We must regulate strip mining of coal to provide satisfactory reclamation, but not to stop production, as half our present coal supply comes from surface mines. We must get new coal mines opened and, for the sake of the consumers, bring the runaway pricing of coal under control.

Our air quality control regulations must be realistic. Ambient standards--the standards that control air quality at ground level--must be met, but emission standards can be given second consideration (at least until technology for sulfur dioxide removal has been proven).

Finally, we must find ways to speed up the licensing and construction of nuclear plants without sacrificing safety standards.

For the long term (to the end of this century), we must rely even more heavily on light-water nuclear reactors like those now being built. We must perfect the nuclear breeder reactor; we must learn how to use coal as a clean fuel; we must develop the fusion reactor, solar energy, and other power sources that offer unlimited supply and even better environmental acceptability. Research in these methods of energy production should be pushed vigorously.

Substitution of electricity for scarce fossil fuels will be part of our long-range energy adjustment. In the years ahead, electricity will carry an increasingly large proportion of the ultimate energy load. Our fossil fuels are bound to become increasingly scarce and higher in price. About 25% of all the energy we consume in this country is now used to generate electricity. It is estimated that, by the end of the century, as much as 50% of our energy will be so used and that perhaps as much as 75% of all our end needs for energy could be met with electricity. In a very real sense, then, electricity is the <u>solution</u> to our energy problem, not a <u>part</u> of it.

This leads to the problems of power supply in the TVA region. The TVA power system is the largest in the United States, with presently over 20 million kilowatts of generating capacity. It is a publicly-owned system responsible for providing power on a self-supporting, nonprofit basis, at the least possible cost to the consumer. More than 80% of its generating capacity is in coal-burning thermal plants, and the rest in hydroelectric generation at large dams. The first nuclear generating unit is just now being tested. When the construction of all nuclear generating units now under way or already purchased is completed, TVA's nuclear capacity will be about 16 million kilowatts, constituting 40% of the total generating capacity.

The power system's two present major problems are fuel supply and fuel cost. For several months, TVA purchasers have been unable to contract for new coal in significant quantities. The system is burning more than it can buy and stockpiles are going down. New mines simply are not being opened. With the increased nationwide demand for coal and with the decreasing supply, the effect on prices has been disastrous for the consumer. As recently as four years ago, the average price TVA paid for coal was about $4.50 per ton. Today it is as much as $11.30 per ton, and reports arrive every day of some buyers paying as much as $20 to $25 per ton.

About half the cost of electricity produced in the TVA system is represented by coal, and its coal bill last year was about $300 million. Unless something is done to stabilize the cost of coal, electric rates are going to rise dramatically. However, TVA power is still a bargain compared with other living costs. In 1940 the average family in the Tennessee Valley spent about 4-1/2% of its family income on power bills; today it is about 2-1/2% while using over ten times as much electricity.

Pocahontas Land Corporation
Bluefield, West Virginia

Coal is America's most abundant natural energy resource. It represents 88% of our known energy fuel reserves and 50% of the world's, yet it supplies only 20% of our nation's energy demands.

Of the 790 billion tons of recoverable coal reserves in the United States, 150 billion tons (19%) are located in Appalachia. Because of its high metallurgical quality, bituminous coal mined in Appalachia is considered to be the finest coking coal in the world and is in high demand for domestic and foreign steel mills.

In 1973 Appalachia supplied approximately three-fourths of all coal produced in the United States. Since coal plays a major role in Appalachia's economy, any changes affecting the coal industry will have a far-reaching effect on the region. For several decades, coal has been a stagnant, secondary industry in our economy. It has been constantly faced with market dislocations and plagued with increasingly stringent and unattainable environmental regulations and an apathetic or even hostile government attitude.

For example, under the Clean Air Act of 1970, large industrial plants using coal were required to reduce their stack emissions to certain levels by July 1, 1975. Since technology for meeting such standards was unavailable, many utilities converted from coal-fired boilers to oil- and gas-fired boilers. The result was a drain on two natural resources already in short supply and continuing market losses for coal.

The Federal Coal Mine Health and Safety Act, which became effective in 1970, brought the coal mining industry additional woes. Although many of the goals of that legislation were admirable, many of the regulations are unrealistic and burdensome. For example, the Act requires that <u>all</u> underground mines install certain "permissible" electrical equipment designed to prevent explosions from the ignition of methane gas by sparks from electrical machinery. Even though methane gas is not present in all underground mines, all mines must comply with the requirement.

Unfortunately, the equipment is too expensive for smaller mining operators and is often unavailable even for those who can afford it. As a result, many mines that do not have the "permissible" equipment will, more than likely, have to shut down. When mines are closed, even for a short period of time, employees take other employment and are not always available if the mines reopen.

Through compliance with the Act, it is estimated that the coal mining industry has suffered a production loss of about 15%-25%. As a result of this loss and of additional labor and supply requirements imposed by the Act, underground mining costs have increased 20%-30%.

Another threat to the viability of the coal industry is House Bill 11500--the proposed Surface Mining Control and Reclamation Act of 1973. Although the Act would permit surface mining, it does so with a number of restrictions that would, in effect, discourage surface mining or make it infeasible. When combined with reasonable reclamation procedures, surface mining can be an asset to both the environment and the economy. It makes possible the recovery of millions of tons of valuable coal that otherwise could not be mined economically and that often could not be mined by any other method. Such mining produces about 50% of our present coal supplies. Surface mining is not only more productive than underground mining but also safer. In 1972 the average tons of coal produced per miner per day through strip mining and auger mining (the two forms of surface mining) were 35.95 and 43, respectively, while underground miners averaged only 11.91 tons per day.

In 1973, of 11,050 nonfatal injuries suffered in mining accidents, 9,450 resulted from underground mining and 1,600 from surface mining; 107 fatalities occurred in underground mining while only 25 resulted from surface mining.

Our present emergency has brought the importance of our coal resources and their use clearly into focus. Our relatively low reserves of energy resources other than coal, the undesirability of depending on foreign fuel, and the staggering balance of payments problem all point to coal as the keystone of our future energy economy.

Coal is now seen as a primary industry, and its development as a national priority. For coal to expand and fulfill this new role, basic changes must be made in the legislative, governmental, environmental, and economic perimeters of the industry.

LENOWISCO* Planning District Commission
Duffield, Virginia 24244

One approach to the energy problem, particularly relevant to Central Appalachia, has not been dealt with extensively. In much of this area, the coal mining industry is the basis of the economy. Certain areas suffered heavy losses when the mining industry began to automate in the early '50s. They could do so again with any major fluctuation in the coal market or in production techniques since they have, as yet, failed to develop a stable economy independent of the mining industry.

Whereas any industry or corporation has a responsibility to its employees and its community, this is particularly true when that industry is the mainstay of the local economy. What happened in coal producing areas in the '50s should never be allowed to happen again. The community and the industry should see to it that they are prepared for fluctuations that can affect a large segment of the community. The locality cannot be prepared for these changes without the cooperation of the mining industry.

This responsibility has been largely ignored by industry, which can no longer be allowed to consider only its own survival. In many parts of Central Appalachia, the coal industry is the lifeblood of the economy, but it is extracting the most valuable resource and transporting it elsewhere for profit. When the coal resources are depleted or no longer in demand, the corporations will move on to other areas, but Appalachia and its people

---

*The Cities of Lee, Norris, Wise, and Scott, Virginia.

will remain, possibly with a shattered economy, a ravaged landscape, and a broken spirit.

We are finally learning that our resources are not infinite, and Appalachia must look to its future. We must do everything in our power to assure that, when the coal mining is gone, we have something left, and that, as long as it is here, the people affected get their fair share. The coal industry must be more open in discussing those aspects of its business that affect the surrounding area, and if the nation wants our coal, we want a larger say in its marketing. The coal industry already has that kind of power, but the people who live with the coal, its benefits and detriments, have little or no say in national policies. We must face our responsibility to Appalachia and ourselves and see to it that those who affect us do likewise.

Mary D. Houska
Associate Professor, Economics
Hollins College, Virginia 24020

This commentary has three parts: (1) an analysis of changes in the energy market; (2) an analysis of the impact on the market for Appalachian coal of any future federal legislation restricting surface mining; and (3) an analysis of the probable impact of the first two on the economy of these mining regions. There are also recommendations for the direction of public policy.

The two major markets for Appalachian coal are metallurgical use and power generation. Much of it has a high BTU content and is a high-carbon, low-to-medium volatile coal. This unique characteristic, plus seams from four to six feet thick, has made this coal the international source for metallurgical purposes. Power generation does not require such a high-grade coal, but a high BTU content is an advantage. Large power plants can switch fuels (from coal to petroleum and vice versa) at will and have done so as the relative cost of these fuels has varied. Furthermore, petroleum may be used for heating operations in metallurgical plants and it is possible to mix the high-carbon coals with lower-quality bituminous.

From 1958 to 1968 the prices of coal and petroleum changed little, and resulted in a sharp recovery of the sales of bituminous coal, reaching a peak in 1970. Then bituminous prices began to rise rapidly and, by December 1972, they were 209.4% of their 1967 level, while domestic refined petroleum prices had increased only 12% over their 1967 level. This sharp price increase caused both total and export bituminous sales to decline steadily, with the domestic output leveling off in late 1973, when the relative price between petroleum and coal had again shifted.

The decline in bituminous output may be due to improved environmental standards for power plants operating in urban areas, but this cannot explain the sharp decline in export sales or the failure of sales of low-sulfur coal to increase. The Japanese market illustrates the impact of these extraordinary price increases on the export sales of U.S. metallurgical coal. In 1970, 50% of the coal imported by Japan came from the United States; in 1973, only 28.2%. Coal imports by Western Europe have followed a similar pattern. Thus it is apparent that the large bituminous price increase in relation to the price of other fuels brought about a substitution of other fuels and a reduction of exports from 1970 to 1973.

These circumstances changed abruptly late in 1973, with heavy cost increases in the use of refined petroleum. The domestic price of petroleum in December 1973 increased 125% over December 1972, while the price of bituminous coal increased only 17% in the same period. The price of petroleum is likely to stabilize at the present higher level. If so, and if the _price_ of coal does not increase appreciably, the _use_ of coal should increase briskly.

The next point to consider is the impact of federal legislation limiting strip mining. In any market, the price of a homogeneous commodity such as coal is determined by its productivity and the cost of producing it, regardless of source. This means that a homogeneous product (e.g., coal of various grades) sold in the same market will have the same market price. Since surface-mined coal has been selling for about 60% of the price of deep-mined coal, we conclude that much of the surface-mined coal is of lower grade than the deep-mined coal and that probably much of it is being sold for local power generation. Certainly, some surface-mined coal is high-grade coal and is apparently being sold to larger deep-mine firms and remarketed at the higher prices.

Sales of metallurgical-grade coal (almost half the Appalachian coal) will not be affected by strip-mine legislation. If the legislation calls for the return of the land to its original contours, cost calculations suggest that profits would be high enough to permit reclamation of surface mines with high-grade seams. If the slope limitations placed on strip mining eliminate Appalachian strip mining, metallurgical coal, at present prices, can be deep-mined at a relatively high profit margin.

The question of the marketing of Appalachian deep-mined coal for Eastern power generation is more complex. If only the higher-grade coal were mined, could it compete with the higher-priced petroleum? It has a higher BTU content than the coal presently used in power generation and much of it is low-sulfur. Should the present price differential between petroleum and coal hold, it is likely that, even with added costs of desulfurizing where necessary and of more stringent enforcement of mine health and safety regulations, deep-mined Appalachian coal of high-quality could be competitive in Eastern markets for power. Much also depends on shipping costs.

At this time, Western coal cannot compete for the Eastern or Mid-Western power generation market, because of its heavier water content and its lower BTU value. It is possible that Western sub-bituminous can be economically converted to manufactured gas and transported by pipeline east of the Mississippi and be price-competitive. A coal-gasification project is now being developed in the Southwest. Gas conversion seems to be the only way that Western coal can compete for Eastern and Mid-Western power generation.

No public data are available estimating probable costs of this conversion or subsequent transportation of the manufactured gas. Because of the depth of the Western coal seams, if this coal is stripped, labor costs and the cost of reclamation are likely to be low per ton. Since the quality of the coal is low, any per-ton added cost (UMWA pension fund contribution or the Seiberling amendment) would have a greater impact on Western than on Appalachian coal. However, any requirements to reclaim Appalachian strip-mining operations similar to the present Pennsylvania law would probably end the stripping of poor quality and/or narrow seams in the Southern Appalachians as well.

Another possible alternative energy source is nuclear power. The higher the cost of petroleum and coal, the better nuclear power will seem. Much, therefore, depends on the relative prices of coal and petroleum, and the price policy is now controlled by the petroleum industry.

Furthermore, as for strip-mining legislation, any law that leads to the elimination of part or all of it would have to allow sufficient lead-time for the reopening of abandoned deep-mine operations and the opening of new ones. It is estimated that one to three years would be necessary for reopened mines to be fully operational and three to five years for new deep mines. Legislation that did not provide for this lead-time would cause extraordinary price increases for Appalachian coal and severely limit its competitive position with Western sub-bituminous or petroleum.

Should legislation pass that gradually limits Eastern stripping but does not eliminate Western surface mining, we can expect the following:

1. an increased use of deep-mined Appalachian coal for Eastern power generation, with some price increase
2. given present Middle Eastern national petroleum policy, the preference of domestic petroleum firms probably to sell this Western coal rather than Middle Eastern petroleum for Eastern power generation (In the long term, they see their most profitable alternative in the development of Western coal reserves and other domestic sources of petroleum.)
3. in about ten years, increased competition for Eastern power generation fuel sources from nuclear energy and gasified Western coal.

The effect on the economy of the Appalachian coal-producing areas should be large employment increases for about ten years. This increase would be derived from both the increase in coal production and the substitution of deep mining for some or all of the surface mining. We have the labor force in the area to fill these new jobs. This employment would generate about one other job in the region for each new job created in mining.

Unfortunately, to date the economy of this region has not benefited from the presence of this valuable resource. By any social or economic measure, the coal mining regions are grossly behind the national average and similar to other isolated rural areas. States and localities should consider a tax to compensate them for the removal of this resource and for any social costs that result from this mining activity.

Technological developments may occur in the next ten years that will help Appalachian coal keep its competitive position. An example is much larger-scale deep mining with at-site coal gasification. The major companies, however, appear to be focusing their research on Western sub-bituminous rather than on Eastern bituminous.

Any future public policy must balance the economic importance of low-cost fuel against the potential environmental damage (both in extraction and use) and the human costs involved. Both the human and long-run environmental and economic costs can be minimized with sound public policy.

Hugh B. Montgomery
The Appalachian Regional Commission

Appalachian rock is rich in entrapped energy--in its coal, petroleum, and natural gas--but the energy of the land, its waters, and its soils interweaves with still another energy--that of the human spirit, an energy of spirit that builds and destroys. In a geologic sense, man's destructive habits are no match for the constructive forces of nature. In a historical sense, so far, man's disruption of the surface exceeds the earth's regenerative powers. Today this imbalance between nature's ways and man's schizophrenic drive to enjoy and destroy brings Appalachia to a crossroads of conscience that tries both the human spirit and the Appalachian land.

Appalachia's bounty is its millstone. Its coal has served the energy markets of the nation and it is expected to deliver even more. Whether or not coal will be supplied from here is not a question, but from exactly where, by what mining methods, at what rate, and for what price are major questions. Who will mine the coal--which corporate superstructures, which local companies, with which miners are also important questions. But the major consideration is "What will Appalachia be like when all of its economically minable coal is gone and no substantial mining industry is left to operate in the coal basin?" The Appalachian Regional Development Act and its administering instrument, the Appalachian Regional Commission, recognize the economic lag and the need to overcome the development deficiences caused both by the collapse of an earlier high level of coal mining activity and by the industry's apparently inherent inability to create a diversified economic structure that can shift to other actions as coal mining periodically subsides. The Appalachian Regional Development program has sought to help the states overcome those economic and social shortfalls that originate partly from the region's strong dependence on an economically and socially inflexible industry. The coal in the ground and its removal have been a qualified asset to Appalachia in the past and will be so in the future. However, the physical, social, and economic scars of the past use of coal and other resources must not be the heritage of the future. Miners should have reasonable health and post-mining economic security. The land and waters should nourish the wildlife and human life after the mining has moved on. The communities' and the state's coal-mining areas must be able to finance their continuing needed services with adequate schools, hospitals, water and sewers, social and artistic outlets, the ability to travel to and from work, and the enjoyments of living.

Man's link with the land determines his well-being. Land can be consumed in the sense that its characteristics can be obliterated, but it can be at least partially recycled. Nature itself recycles land, moves it about, reorders its characteristics, redresses it in greenery, and repopulates it with living creatures. Man should respect these processes. Energy extracted from the ground and moved about requires the digging of mines, wells, and shafts at the surface and subsurface, and rights-of-way cut swaths across the land for highways, service roads, railroads, pipelines, powerlines, and waterways. As energy is produced and moved around the country in larger quantities, more of these diggings can be expected and will require even more attention to the consumption of the quantities and qualities of land, water, air, and wildlife.

Furthermore, men will also continue to use convenient or available land that is subject to energy disorders of natural or man-stimulated hazards such as landslides, surface collapse, and flooding. The Appalachian Regional program has recognized the states' interests and needs in land use. It has served as a medium for defining and developing new ideas and the means for coping with the organization and financing of natural-hazards prevention and recovery from catastrophes. Looking ahead, as the population grows, as energy is developed, and as the land is re-formed to accommodate man's growth, we must develop a general land and wildlife ethic among our adults and young so that they can manage the limits of the earth as well as its bounties. Such an ethic should also be the foundation of economic development and governmental institutions serving the peoples' survival and well-being as it is vested in all of the land, regardless of ownership.

Although the earth has always been bountiful, man must win the bounty. During the winning, he learns to love that land and develops a spiritual relationship with it. If his relationship to the land is rewarding, his community benefits from a full human spirit.

Within the community, men can work together in ways most fulfilling to all. Chief among man's tools, outside of his constructive individuality, is that he can guide and settle matters of common concern. The clans of old were founded and perpetuated on leadership, respect, and structured relationships. Pride in these relationships added to the satisfaction of a fulfilled human spirit. In our time, our clannishness has given us government that can also be a just vehicle for insuring a satisfied human spirit. The Appalachian Regional Commission is only one useful expression of this. Individuality can bring us much, but working together can compound the rewards. What we cannot do for ourselves, we must look for from our family, friends, and government. The tolerating, in the governmental process, of inadequate officialdom or questionable loyalties can and must be resolved by each man expressing his interests on his own behalf. The Appalachian Regional Commission is a government instrument of the people. All of the people of the nation share in its federal aspect, and all the people of the thirteen Appalachian states share in its state aspects. The future demands much of Appalachia's energy resources, its land, and, most of all, its people.

Many have attempted to define a quality of life. It requires of every man (in government or in private) the intent to seek a full reward from the land, while assuring future generations an Appalachia worth inheriting.

Second Session: LAND USE

Of the several exhibits illustrating Appalachian life, the documentary "Appalachian Genesis" showed the effects of current exploitations on the young people. It showed how they lacked the small graces and comforts that most Americans take for granted, such as adequate education and basic medical services. The movie related these lacks to the effects of strip mining on the land and of deep mining on the people.

The next movie showed how road building, generally considered a public good, can affect the land nearly as badly as strip mining. The moral, though unspoken, appeared to be that both road builders and miners should select their sites with greater care, determine ahead of time whether reclamation is possible, and attend to the restoration of the scarred land immediately.

A third movie, "The Region--in Change," examined the impact of change on the environment of the Southern Highlands area as voiced by local citizens and officials. They questioned the present system of values and development processes, especially as practiced in the resort areas and second-home communities.

The subsequent concurrent sessions on land use raised more questions than they answered. The proposed solutions ranged from strictly local determinations through a regional land-use policy to areas totally and deliberately denuded by technology.

If the reader will keep in mind that no one item can be neatly separated from energy requirements and the needs of the human spirit, herewith are comments, opinions, and queries on the vexacious subject of land use.

We must be aware of the shocks--both cultural and agricultural--of development. Growth is not necessarily good; material possessions do not necessarily lead to a better life. The medieval notion that man holds dominion over all he surveys is no longer upheld; on the contrary, he seems to be a misfit in the ecosystem, both naturally and socially. He puts buildings on the most fertile land and will soon have no more food land. He has established an adversary relationship between the developers and the long-range inhabitants for the benefit of the outlanders, e.g., campers, seasonal recreation users, and summer home owners.

Public support is needed to inspire communities to petition for strict local zoning laws instead of following easy state standards. Such zoning could prevent the growth of industry along highways (especially the Blue Ridge Parkway) and confine it to the fringe areas of towns. Good land would thus be saved for agriculture and its related industries. Careful zoning would also eliminate high-density building by demanding adequate sewerage and minimum-sized lots, and would keep developers off the tops of ridges by requiring good sewerage systems, access roads, water and power supply, and erosion control. As conditions change, the zoning code would have to be reviewed regularly, of course, to see that no one man was locked into a life of sheep-raising while his neighbor was allowed to sell his land for quick profit.

Taxation, too, could be used to offset misuse of land. The concept of private property has been considered unassailable and its ownership has admitted little or no responsibility for its misuse. This concept is now showing signs of erosion, even of revision. A recognition of public welfare, neighbors' or descendants' rights, utility, and justice is emerging, albeit slowly. (After all, private business is unlikely soon to curtail its own profits.) When private property is taxed, its true cost to the community should be considered, e.g., poor access roads, overuse of existing roads, uncontrolled runoff, and the like. Where possible, taxes should be heavier on projects that drain off municipal funds or deplete local resources and progressively lighter on those that do not do so.*

The Appalachian citizens appear to need a Bill of Rights. Who, for instance, decides where energy sites are to go? Who insists on the reclamation of the devastation? The people need to be educated to _want_ reform, to ask for a regional assessment of their environment, to demand a reorganization of their tax structure that will reflect a true best use of their land, not just the most profitable one. In short, they must find some one or some agency that will understand and work for those most affected. Such funds for local use will undoubtedly have to come from the federal government. The greatest frustration is where to start.

---

*In spite of these zoning and tax precautions, the regional folk life is bound to be eroded by modern education, the influx of tourists, and voluntary emigration.

The process of democracy is related to a Bill of Rights for citizens. It is exceedingly slow and the time for conservation is rapidly running out. As with depressed people generally, the mountaineers are inclined to re-elect those who preserve their misery. (They distrust the federal government, in spite of its abundance of funds, for its custom of riding over everything local in its path.) Occasionally, both strict zoning and corrective taxation meet head-on with local practical politics. The local incumbent may be willing to press for either or both, but, if he should pinch off someone's immediate profit, he may not be re-elected. All this politician can do is hope that his electorate will see the wisdom of such a course and actually come to request it. Some Appalachians no longer wish to be "folks"--alternately exploited or patronized--but to be world citizens, weighing local needs against national and international needs. The frustration, again, is where to start.

As resource use rises and benefits diminish, technology becomes demonstrably untrustworthy. Recreation and tourism have been satisfactory for some sections such as the reforested areas. (Absentee owners do pay relatively high taxes for slight tax use.) Little account, however, has been taken of the fact that industrialization affects urban areas differently from rural areas. In urban areas, local technicians are employed while, in the rural areas, few or no technicians are trained; instead the local citizens are given only unskilled or semi-skilled jobs in the factories and tourist complexes.

A special example of technocracy in action is the Tennessee Valley Authority, which has both benefited and distorted the area. It has taught the inhabitants good resource husbandry and provided cheap power, but its flood control dams use the fertile flat lands and displace the people. Following its mandate to provide cheap power, it has used strip-mined coal for its low cost, but has had questionable success in reclamation.

As for the use of the forest lands it seems that the effects of overcutting are much the same as for strip mining. State forest services provide advice on the proper use of timber land, but only on request. The U.S. Forest Service's long-range planning concentrates on sustained-yield management, which takes account of the ecological balance--wildlife, watershed, soil, flora, etc. It includes both regenerative and intermediate thinnings, followed by planting or seeding and encouragement of natural regeneration.

Assignment of land for parks and recreation is a heartening project, especially if recreation is considered in its broadest sense, namely as re-creation, not as duplication of the comforts of home. The human spirit would indeed be refreshed by visits to true wilderness areas. Cluster building in resort areas would preserve more of the wild surroundings by limiting the intensity of development to a level tolerable to the fragile environment. Urban centers could also profit from a variety of parks; bike trails, picnic areas, and green islands in shopping malls are only three examples. Support must be found for local and regional zoning laws and for subdivision regulations that favor the best recreational land use and expansion, especially in local communities.

If any or all of the foregoing land-use plans are not used soon, man may be driven to the most radical solution of all--selective technical denudation.* Our current random destruction would be replaced, through ultra-long-range planning, by the choice of specific areas of the world for total consumption of the earth's crust. This would mean the use of all material, to and through bedrock, at this site and would have the advantage of confining the blight and pollution within its own boundaries. As the particular area was being systematically denuded, its surface resources (timber, farmland, etc.) would be re-established elsewhere.

One summation of the land-use ideal was given as "land planning from local to state to national to world--with emphasis on the unique at each stage."

The following precis of position papers elaborate on the points made above.

---

*Robert E. Reiman. "Environmental Heresy: Ultra-long-range Planning for Technological Denudation." Boone, N.C.: Appalachian State University, 1974.

LAND USE

American Petroleum Institute
1801 K Street, N.W.
Washington, D.C. 20006

Second only to the talents and energies of her citizens, America's most valuable resource is the land, but, in an age of rapidly expanding industrialization and urbanization, we have almost lost sight of this fact. As a result, far-reaching decisions on the use of land are being made with too little thought for their ultimate effects on our entire way of life. It is impossible to over-estimate the need for policies that insure wise use of land.

The current shortage of available energy is perhaps the best example of what can result from inadequate land planning. All but a small fraction of our energy needs are met by fuels extracted from the ground. Although energy and land are inseparable, the development, generation, and transmission of energy have been severely limited by inappropriate land-use policies. For example, it is becoming increasingly difficult to find suitable sites for petroleum refineries and deepwater terminals along our Eastern seaboard, where they are critically needed. One state has prohibited all petroleum development in or near its coastal zone and similar legislation has been proposed in other states. The expansion of off-shore oil production, which has been found after careful study to be environmentally acceptable and is urgently needed to increase domestic energy self-sufficiency, will be impossible if states prohibit the construction of pipeline and storage facilities onshore.

Industry cannot bring new oil supplies from the ground unless it has access to the land; it cannot transport the crude oil to refineries unless pipelines and related facilities are permitted; it cannot refine the crude oil unless refinery sites are provided for; and it cannot move the finished products to consumers unless the transportation network is available.

The failure of many states and localities to consider the need for energy has inhibited the consumer's ability to obtain the fuel he needs to heat and light his home, to power his factories, and to run his vehicles. The needs for energy facilities--needs clearly national in character--are inseparable from land. The failure of land-use plans to provide adequate domestic energy can lead only to increased dependence on foreign sources, to the dangers of even more serious supply interruptions than already experienced, and to rapid price increases. The United States would find it difficult to pursue an independent foreign policy, and its economy would be marred by the heavy expense of massive imports. Energy self-sufficiency is a high national priority.

While energy industries must be permitted access to the land, they must recognize that in past years they have given insufficient attention to preservation of the environment. Probably the most glaring example of this short-sighted approach is in Appalachia itself, where strip mining of coal on steep slopes and insufficient attention to reclamation resulted in serious damage to the land and in pollution of rivers and streams. Fortunately, laws now exist to assure the continued preservation and restoration of ecological balance.

Economic development (including energy development) and environmental integrity are not mutually exclusive goals. Land-use policies should be flexible to accommodate changing national growth patterns, technological advances, and economic needs, while assuring the maintenance of a healthy environment. Through careful land-use planning, we can conserve environmental values and still provide the energy to meet the growing demands of the consuming public and a healthy economy.

F. Schmidt-Bleek
Environment Center
University of Tennessee
Knoxville, Tennessee

We must reconcile our energy needs with protection of the environment. We are talking about the quality of life--about being healthy and warm, and having transportation, about power and the goods we need without drowning in pollution. Energy is a key factor in the quality of life, as the American people have begun to realize, but it will take a good deal of energy to protect us from the negative impact of producing energy.

Coal is the energy source with which we at the University of Tennessee Environment Center are most concerned. In the mining of coal, in both deep mines and strip mines, we incur quantifiable, measurable, and considerable environmental impact. The major thrust of our coal research project is to find out just how expensive and extensive these environmental damages are.

Some of the obvious damages from deep mines include slag piles and contamination of streams. One effect, not so obvious, is the high incidence of death, disease, and injury to the miners. No other occupation is as hazardous.

In Central Appalachian surface mining, the greatest impact is from the large land area involved. Typically, two to three acres of surface are disturbed for the production of 5000 tons of coal. Water quality is sharply affected, and water run-off problems lead to considerably increased flooding. Topography is changed and, in some cases, entire mountain tops are removed. Possibly the damage most difficult to calculate is the visual damage. It is fair to say that 50% to 70% of Central Appalachia has been visually affected by strip mining.

We need more coal--and we can get it and still repair the damage caused by mining. More input in machinery, capital, and manpower will be required. Environmental restoration will necessarily increase the cost of coal, and the price of coal products, e.g., electricity. In the mass media and in announcements by the energy industry, such price increases are frequently portrayed as enormous, but very adequate restoration of surface mines, for example, would increase the electricity end-price by only 5%. This seems rather insignificant compared to the enormous price increases TVA, for instance, has posted during the last 24 months.

It is a mistake to think that the environment is going to "wait" until we decide to go back and repair the damage. The fact is that people who live in the mining areas are already experiencing costs as a result of the mining activity. Their lands are flooded, their agricultural activity is hurt, the visual beauty of the landscape is destroyed. These real costs are being borne by those least able to stand them--the residents of the affected areas.

The cost should be borne by those who benefit from the use of a product--in this case, energy. We must make a serious effort to identify these damages and repair them, not just continue to behave as if the costs are imaginary and, after some catastrophe, scramble to patch things up. If we do not take care of environmental costs as early and as efficiently as possible, they will increase very steeply. We must try to recognize the true costs and make wise decisions on how to meet them. Otherwise, these costs we have been piling up will have to be paid all at once.

For years now, our energy has been cheap and apparently plentiful, and the cost of providing environmental protection has seemed large in comparison. Because of increased demand on the one hand and decreased supply on the other, the costs of all kinds of energy are going to rise sharply and, in the future, environmental protection may not seem so prohibitively expensive.

At any rate, it is time to talk in rational, dollars-and-cents terms about total costs and benefits and about how to distribute them. It is time to understand environmental damages as real costs and let them be reflected in realistic end-prices of goods and services.

American consumers should have the right to make this decision, and should not continue to be fooled by pricing mechanisms that are bound to spring extremely unpleasant surprises on them from time to time.

Louis H. Hunter, Executive Vice President
National Independent Coal Operators' Association
Richlands, Virginia 24621

If land was put on earth to be used by man, we should remove the natural resources, put them to their best use, and put the land back to a more productive state. The coal should be mined by safer methods, more economically, for a better environment, and with good reclamation. Appalachia needs more industry, and more land for homes, schools, churches, gardening, and many other things. This can be accomplished by proper, well planned surface mining of coal, especially in very steep terrain in certain areas, keeping in mind successful reclamation. In recent years a college, large elementary schools, airports, greenhouses, industrial plants, small farms, and many expensive homes have been built on reclaimed, surface-mined land in Appalachia and this can continue in the future. If it had not been surface-mined, it would remain a steep terrain of little or no use except for growing timber (of use a hundred years from now).

With the shortages of today, we (worldwide) will more than likely have a food shortage, and all land will be needed for raising food for the hungry. The surface-mine benches left in the steep terrain, in addition to raising food, are useful for raising cattle and sheep, and are good for wild game. Many productive orchards and berry patches have been planted on surface benches.

In Switzerland, Austria, and other European countries, the people reside on the side of the mountains and use the flat lands for farming only because the mountains are too steep for farming. In the Appalachian mountains, many small farms are being made by surface mining.

With proper grading, these surface-mined areas can prevent land erosion and the washing of silt and topsoil down into the streams, although silt and topsoil washed into the streams can be very useful. The lowlands along the rivers have been fertilized by flooding for many years, long before surface mining of coal and other minerals was even thought of.

It has been suggested at various times that the abandoned underground mines might be used for burial grounds, for storage, for aging of cheese and other foods that need even temperatures, or for garbage disposal.

Recently an attorney at a surface-mine hearing stated that he purchased 500 acres of mountain land (without an access road) for $7,500 ($15.00 per acre). After this land, which is of steep terrain, is surface-mined and reclaimed, he plans to sell it for $80,000 to $100,000 for housing developments.

Land use should be controlled by local and state, not federal, government because every locality has different soil and terrain. The proper way to use land in North Carolina and Virginia would be entirely different from Colorado and California, especially for land reclamation. We should be permitted to use our land as we see fit, rather than have someone else come in and tell us what to do.

Tennessee Valley Authority
Knoxville, Tennessee 37902

Beginning with the congressional deliberations that established TVA, wise use of land, including reestablishing the valley's badly eroded land base, was a central goal in its program for regional development. It was needed to overcome the economic and social troubles stemming from the ravaged land.

Early TVA activities supplied the system of dams and reservoirs to reduce river flooding, creating protected land areas for settlement and other productive uses. The system also maintains sustained streamflows and assures water for domestic, industrial, and recreational purposes. Erosion of the land base was attacked through reforestation, reduction of fire damage, and improved forest management. Better soil management was achieved through promotion of the shift from row crops to pasture and other agricultural methods calculated to reduce erosion. Through the work of the National Fertilizer Development Center and cooperating state agencies, increased crop yields and improved agricultural practices have been realized both in the Tennessee Valley and throughout the nation.

Other tools were provided to aid economic growth, including a commercially navigable Tennessee waterway and the TVA power system. These and other available resources enabled the region to begin developing the economic base needed for balanced regional growth.

Community development has also been a TVA objective, and technical assistance in planning is one of the tools it has made available. The Norris new-town experiment was undertaken to test new ideas in community living and to demonstrate an alternative to large urban areas as human living environments. Under its tributary area-development, Townlift, community-improvement programs, TVA has made available to participating communities many kinds of special assistance. Maps and data on flood hazards have enabled many communities to develop and enforce appropriate land-use regulations to avoid damage in flood plain areas. Using these tools, the Tennessee Valley region during the last 40 years has evolved from an under-producing agricultural region to an urban-industrial economy, with widespread community development and accompanying land-use problems.

Today the urban pattern of the valley can best be described as a system of cities, ranging from communities of 50,000 to a few hundred people. An improved transportation system links these communities and makes possible considerable interaction among them.

A special feature of the Tennessee Valley region during the 1960s, unlike the nation as a whole, was that a greater share of the region's growth occurred in the small- and medium-sized communities. While this small-town growth offers a choice of environment to valley residents, it will also tend to increase pressures on the valley's land base. As the small- and medium-sized towns increase in number and size, and as rural growth occurs there will be increased competition for the use of land. Land-use changes in wildlife, recreation and forest areas, prime agricultural lands, flood plains, and natural areas are likely to become more frequent and controversial.

A related matter is the need to provide locations for facilities vital to the continued growth of the region--for example, power plants, power transmission corridors, and transportation facilities (highways, railroads, and airports).

In adjusting to these changing conditions and to the needs of regional growth, we will need new approaches. Land-resource management is primarily a regional problem, and a regional problem-solving framework is needed. In the American system, state government is the principal regional governmental unit.

A primary state objective in developing and carrying out a land-use planning program should be to promote economic growth and the protection of the human environment. This objective should be based on an understanding of environmental tolerances, land capabilities, and the needs of people.

Further, technology must be used to help supply solutions to problems created by an urban society. For example, technology is particularly important in assuring air and water quality, in providing for waste disposal; and the location and operation of power plants and other energy sources require technological assurances that the human environment will not be diminished.

In addition, the state land-use planning program should provide for the use of special techniques for managing human needs. For example, new town developments should be guided, and modernization of older communities and revitalization of others should produce attractive and efficient places to live and work.

Also in state land use, the value of the land for irreplaceable primary production such as minerals, food and fiber, and scenic beauty should be protected. In spite of the growth and visibility of nonfarm-related industry, farm-dependent business remains a viable segment of the economy, and farming an important source of income. Growth that depends on land primarily for space should be guided to areas that interfere minimally with the use of land for primary production or to compatible joint uses of land, such as disposal of urban wastes to rehabilitate strip-mined land or as a soil conditioner on farm lands.

Technical assistance, drawing on TVA's multipurpose program and on information in a variety of functional areas related to land-use planning, is available to the states. TVA help in mapping, power plant siting, industrial park location and design, recreation planning, and community improvement are just a few examples of where collaboration can bring about better overall land-use planning. TVA will also continue to take on problem-solving activities involving more than one state.

Dennis C. Shultz
Sierra Club
Matthews, North Carolina

"Strip Mining Can Be Made Acceptable," said a headline over the comments of W.J. Burton of Duke Power Company in The Charlotte Observer of March 12, 1974.

That headline is correct. Strip mining is already acceptable. It is acceptable to Duke Power, Consolidated Coal, the American Mining Congress, and others who expound cheap power without regard for tomorrow, as has been demonstrated by the continuing rape of the Appalachian mountains.

The question really is whether strip mining can be made acceptable to the people who live in Appalachia, to those who love the hills, to those who live downstream on acidic and polluted rivers, to the 188 persons who lost their lives when a mine dam burst on Buffalo Creek in West Virginia, and to the future generations who will be forced to live among denuded hills, silt-choked, acidic rivers, and barren rock walls, and obliged to carry the burden of supporting a geographic area that has been physically and economically stripped.

I hoped Mr. Burton would reveal how this might be accomplished. To my dismay, there was not a word about how Duke Power activities were to make strip mining "more acceptable." It appears that Duke is taking the position of talking the problem away with public relations rather than by facing it directly.

What effort is Duke expending toward the reclamation of strip mines? How many professionals in mining engineering, forestry, hydrology, geology, or agronomy are employed for this objective? How does this budget compare with advertising, public relations, lobbying, and other activities that add to Duke's expenses without directly contributing to the generation of power?

This problem is more immediately serious than coal costs. We, as responsible people, are charged with the stewardship of this land, which means that, despite fee titles and documents of ownership for today, we must shape the land legacy of our descendants.

Severe regulatory legislation is the product of abuse, a form of coercion necessary to reestablish balance. Responsibility is not a product of coercion and, until responsibility is demonstrated, it will be necessary to force compliance with reasonable expectations of responsibility by legislation.

Mr. Burton notes that strip mining is cheaper than deep mining. It would seem only reasonable that some portion of this differential be used to prevent acid drainage, siltation, and gross negligence of the stripped areas. This would still be compatible with avoiding deep mining because of its hazards and cost. The total economic and social costs associated with strip mining are not too well known. The reason is simple: American mining practices have been traditionally based on exploitation, not on conservation.

To understand the degree of this exploitation, consider how little is spent to protect the environment. Coal can be stripped at an estimated $1.50 per ton less than deep-mined coal. Based on a productivity of 3,500 to 5,000 tons per acre, which is common in the East, the $200- to $500-per-acre spent on reclamation (as estimated by TVA) amounts to 10 cents per ton for the environment. If this were increased to $1.00 per ton, it would still be competitive with deep-mined coal.

In West Germany and Great Britain, where land stewardship is taken seriously, this is exactly what is being spent on reclamation. Why can we not learn from their experience? Must we wait until there is no recourse? As the article states, it is possible to reclaim <u>some</u> of the land to productive use, implying that some of the land <u>cannot</u> be restored.

I understand that the bill originally co-sponsored by Representative Jim Martin was simply to prevent mining of nonrestorable land and insure restoration where possible. How can Mr. Burton object to this approach, if he accepts the premise that strip mining must be "made acceptable"? The question is, to whom?

Duke Power Company
Charlotte, North Carolina 28201

Duke Power Company owns thousands of acres in North and South Carolina, with a wide variety of environments from mountains to swamps, from city business districts to remote forest coves. The uses of the land are also varied--power generating plants, water reservoirs, watershed forests, marinas, transmission lines, coal mines, et cetera.

Only land, of all the tangible possessions of man, is unique. This uniqueness gives land use the highest priority. The basic principle that guides all land use by Duke Power is that it must be used in a way that will improve the quality of life for the affected community. Decisions on land use for any particular location require both subjective and objective evaluations. In recent years, knowledge of the environmental sciences has expanded greatly, reducing the degree of subjectivity in decisions on land use, but it is far less than needed to eliminate it.

From this background, let us consider the major kinds of land use in which Duke Power Company is involved.

1. Traditionally, Duke's power plant siting program has focused on large generating complexes, which often bring together in one area several feasible electrical energy generating modes. Lake Norman and the Keowee-Toxaway Project are examples of this long-range planning. Recent regulatory changes have necessitated selection of more geographically diversified sites, but such sites undergo the same intensive investigation as do sites of long-standing public record. Power plants require use of air, land, and water resources. Sites are selected after thorough consideration of social and economic

factors, physical characteristics, and environmental impact. Duke is committed to locating its power facilities so as to maintain and enhance the quality of life in its service area to the maximum practical extent and in compliance with all governing state and federal regulations.

2. Obviously, power generating facilities must be linked with transmission and distribution lines to serve the more than one million customers in Duke's service area. Transmission-line routing is a product of detailed studies similar to those made for plant sites, and results in a prime route and several alternative routes.

3. The main reason for Duke Power to construct a water reservoir is the generation of electrical energy. The energy developed in the head of impounded water is converted into electricity and/or the impounded water is a vehicle to return accumulated waste heat to the natural environment in a diluted form over an extended period of time. Water reservoirs require large areas of land; therefore Duke Power believes it is wise land-use policy to expend additional funds and effort to maximize public use of the water for recreation (consistent with the primary hydroelectric purposes).

4. Generating plants require energy in the form of fossil or nuclear fuels. Duke Power owns land on which the immediate use is mineral extraction or coal mining by surface and deep mining. Since coal can be mined only where it occurs, the land use is dictated. However, mining is only one phase of land use. If mining of coal is a valid

use of land, its reclamation for future production and use is equally important.

5. Duke Power owns land that is not used for plant sites, water reservoirs, or coal mining, but is typical rural real estate. We call it "non-utility land." Location, access, and amenities are the principal factors governing the use of non-utility land. Most of it has been developed for commercial timber and watershed protection. Commercial timber forests are used to provide additional recreation opportunities for the public and, through leases with state agencies, to promote growth of wildlife.

6. Certain small parcels of non-utility land are subject to intensive man-made developments. Decisions for land use in these cases are based mostly on social and economic considerations. Land use in the immediate neighborhood of a site is important. In some situations, the social factor takes precedence over the economic factor.

Land use decisions require the utmost in careful fact-gathering and analysis. Duke Power attempts to use its land in an orderly system that produces the most benefit without waste, protects critical pieces of land, and includes information and opinion from many disciplines.

Pocahontas Land Corporation
Bluefield, West Virginia

The term "land use" has many connotations, ranging from a farmer's rotating his crops to obtain maximum benefits from the soil to a government's regulation of certain land for specific purposes, i.e., residential, industrial, public. Because of the rugged topography of Appalachia, land use in that region is frequently thought of as synonymous with mining. Many areas are unsuitable for any other purpose, and land level enough for farming, industry, and homes is both scarce and expensive.

Roads and railroads cost from three to five times more to build in the mountainous region of Appalachia than in level areas of nearby states and are generally confined to narrow valley floors. Access roads are few, and many small communities are isolated even though only a few miles from large cities.

Timber, oil, and gas are important resources in Appalachia, but coal is the most plentiful. As a result, coal mining plays a major role in Appalachia's economy, bringing boom and recession periods as markets rise and fall.

Of the two basic methods used to recover coal, surface mining is the more controversial. It began in the mountainous areas of Appalachia during World War II under few restrictions or regulations. At a time when manpower was scarce and quick recovery of coal was vital to the nation's welfare, surface mining offered a quick solution to an energy problem. In addition, many coal deposits that were not recoverable through conventional underground mining became available through the surface method. A minimum of preparation, manpower, and investment was needed, and the percentage of coal recovery was high. Unfortunately, however, after such mining was completed, few efforts were made to reclaim the land.

Such irresponsible use of the land brought a host of problems: soil erosion, landslides, stream pollution, floods, and resentment from residents and conservationists--associations that are still difficult to live down. As a result, many people today still think of surface mining as it was in that era and fail to see that, when accompanied by conscientious planning and reclamation programs, it can exemplify good land use in its fullest sense. Not only does the process yield mineral resources but it may also make the land more useful and valuable than it was before mining.

Advanced planning and improved methods are breaking surface mining away from its shadowy past. For example, in a new approach to surface mining called box-cut back-hauling, all the earth that is removed from a cut made perpendicular to contour is redistributed or back-hauled into the preceding cavity or cut. Instead of soil being shoved over the mountainside it is restored to approximate the original contour. High walls are either reduced or nonexistent, and vegetation can be grown on the entire site. Another new approach is the mountaintop-valley-fill method. As its name implies, the entire mountaintop is removed down to a coal bed and the resultant overburden is placed in an adjacent valley. After mining, large plateaus of usable land have been created.

Reclamation of surface-mined land has come a long way. No longer is the mere tossing of grass seed and the random planting of trees acceptable. Land reclamation has become a science, with the grading of land and the selection of vegetation tailored precisely to a particular environment. Mountain terrain formerly too rugged for any use but mining can be and has been converted into timber forests, lakes stocked with fish, grazing pastures for cattle, agricultural land, and flat areas suitable for homes and industry.

In a region where level land is at a premium, proper surface mining and land reclamation offer residents of Appalachia valuable acreage and an opportunity for a better way of life.

Richard Cartwright Austin, Co-Chairman
COALition Against Strip Mining
Washington, D.C. 20003

The new concern for energy and for the productivity of our land strengthens the position of the COALition Against Strip Mining. Strip mining should be phased out in an orderly manner in favor of expanded underground mining. This would develop the mining methods that can reach all our coal resources, including our abundant low-sulphur resources. It would also enable our ranchlands to raise meat, our farmlands to raise other food, and our Appalachian hardwood forests to raise timber. It would protect surface owners from the destruction of their property, and residents of the coalfields generally from sliding mountains and flooding streams. It would rebuild the coal industry nearer to what is needed and reduce transportation costs and transmission inefficiencies. Rebuilding underground mining could provide 100,000 new jobs where they are both needed and wanted--some in the West, more in the Midwest, most in the depressed Appalachian mountains.

Three years ago, the national debate on strip mining stressed the environmental consequences of stripping and the damage to people and property. In the past year, attention has shifted to the question of how to obtain adequate energy supplies and still protect the productive capacity of timberlands, farmlands, and ranchlands. We have discovered that meat, other food, lumber, and energy are all in short supply.

During this period, Congress has been considering legislation to regulate strip mining for coal. The Senate passed its Bill S425, in the first session of the present Congress. The House is currently considering its version, HR11500. Federal strip-mining legislation may give citizens important new tools to fight for adequate reclamation, but it will not win the struggle by itself. The legislation may provide means for banning strip mining in certain critical areas. It could abort the present plans of the energy industry and the Nixon administration to shift coal mining from Eastern deep mining to Western strip-mining where windfall profits can be made. It is on this point that the toughest fights remain.

Up to now, a cautious Congress has been reluctant to ban strip mining altogether, but as it continues to replace deep mining, and as mining investment shifts from the East to the West, it is becoming apparent to more congressmen that these trends are destroying valuable lands while actually decreasing our capacity to use coal as a long-term energy resource.

THE COAL IS DEEP. Using today's methods, there is eight times as much coal available for underground mining as for strip mining. As technologies improve and energy prices rise so that more coal reserves become profitable to mine, there will be 33 times as much coal available to deep mining as to stripping. Strippable reserves will be exhausted in some Appalachian states in one decade, but there is enough low-sulphur, deep-minable coal in Appalachia alone to last this country for several decades. When technologies develop for the cleaner use of high-sulphur coals, the supply will become virtually unlimited. Coal is our nation's only truly abundant fossil fuel.

The trend has been away from deep mining because strip mining has been more profitable to the operator. He has not had to pay for the long-term destruction of the productivity of the 3,000 square miles of America already stripped for coal. Deep-mine production and employment have dropped in the past decade. Squeezed by the competition, underground mines have cut corners at the expense of the health and safety of the miners.

PRODUCTIVE, SAFE MINING. American underground mining technology is antiquated by world standards and the mines are unnecessarily hazardous because the energy industry has not been investing in underground research, development, and capital improvements. New methods, such as longwall mining, could remove 90% of the coal seam, double productivity, and greatly increase mine safety. A new government project has demonstrated that explosive methane gas can be piped from the coal seam in advance of mining. This not only improves safety, but will also, over time, nearly double our reserves of natural gas. Such developments can help make 18 billion tons of low-sulphur, high-energy coal available in Appalachia alone. This is thirty times as much as our total annual coal production.

THE RACE WEST TO POOR COAL. Nevertheless, the largest coal companies are in a race to the West even though the major demands for coal and electricity from coal remain in the East. Western coal and lignite are generally of poor quality, having about half the energy per ton of Eastern coal, but stripping the very thick seams under the farms and ranches is so cheap and easy that a quick profit can be made. It takes a lot of energy (diesel oil and electricity) to operate the big machines that dig the coal. More energy is lost in thousand-mile transmission lines or expended for unit-train trips from Montana to Chicago to deliver low-energy coal, but these costs (and resulting shortages) would be passed on to the consumer through the utilities' rate structures.

The people of the West don't want to be stripped. The people of Appalachia don't want to lose their major industry. The shift West is an inefficient way to obtain increased energy for our country. Nevertheless the shift is under way because capital investment in Western stripping brings a quicker return.

DEEP MINE RESEARCH. The implications of these facts were beginning to dawn as the full Senate debated the strip mining bill last October. On the floor, the findings of the bill were amended to state that "the overwhelming percentage of the nation's coal reserves can only be extracted by underground mining methods, and it is, therefore, essential to the national interest to insure the existence of an expanding and economically healthy underground coal-mining industry." The purpose of the bill was strengthened to "encourage the full utilization of coal resources through the development and application of underground extraction technologies." The Mansfield amendment was added to halt the development of stripping of federal coal under private surface in the West; this would remove a significant portion of Western coal reserves from surface exploitation and slow the present movement to the West. And $20 million were authorized for coal research and demonstration projects for "coal mining technologies which provide alternatives to surface disturbance and which maximize the recovery of available coal resources, including the improvement of present underground mining wastes to the mine void, methods for the underground mining of thick seams and very deep coal seams . . . and safety and health in the application of such technologies. . . ."

SEIBERLING AMENDMENT. In November the House sub-committees went further and added the Seiberling amendment to the House bill in an attempt to redress the economics that presently favor strip mining over deep mining, at the expense of the land. This amendment would fund a program to reclaim previously stripped lands through a fee of $2.50 per ton on every ton of coal mined by any method. Before paying the fee, strippers could deduct their actual costs of reclamation, while deep mine operators could deduct the costs of health and safety equipment required by the Coal Mine Health and Safety Act of 1969, plus the costs of black lung benefits also required by that law. The net effect of the fee, minus the deductions, would be to add about 25¢ a ton to the cost of deep mining, to add about $1.50 a ton to the cost of Eastern stripping, and to add about $2.25 a ton to the cost of Western stripping. This would make deep mining competitive with strip mining again, and enhance the economic incentives toward the development of new deep mines, which will be more useful in building a long-term capacity to meet our energy needs. Deep mines will also provide more employment and do less environmental damage.

The vast Western reserves of low-grade coals and lignite can be developed usefully when technologies such as underground gasification are perfected to remove the energy in large quantities without disturbing the surface. It is folly to use today's primitive technologies--strip mines, steam plants, transmission lines, unit trains--to move Western energy inefficiently to the East and to destroy much of the West in the bargain.

The Seiberling amendment and similar initiatives are being opposed vigorously by the energy industry--and by its bought-and-paid-for Nixon administration--because these proposals would upset the speculative investments that have been moving to Western strip mining. It is around these issues that the most intense battles will be waged as the House completes work on the strip-mining bill.

LENOWISCO* Planning District Commission
Duffield, Virginia

The development of regional planning in Appalachia has only recently, and quite belatedly, recognized the necessity for land planning. Broadly speaking, activity in recent years has centered around the stabilization of Appalachia, with an emphasis on economic development, flood control, and transportation. Appalachian program development and activity have lacked broad goals to provide the needed direction for the basic finite resources, among them the land base. Consequently, it is imperative that land planning be included in this stabilization process. Furthermore, national and regional developmental policies must be clarified and adopted, and a concerted effort made to apply them in our day-to-day decision making. Regional planning can contribute in this effort.

Many will ask if regional planning as a concept has a role in this process of land planning. The answer of those who work in regional agencies is clear. A broader interpretation, however, is given by decision makers at the national, state, and local levels.

Here we find an increasingly greater thrust towards regionalism, especially in land planning. Therefore, to a significant extent the role of regional planning agencies in land-use planning is being formulated by other segments of the American system. It is suggested that the _scale_ at which regional planning functions is a major reason it is being looked upon

---

*The Cities of Lee, Norris, Wise, and Scott, Virginia

as a mechanism that can make concerted efforts in applying policies in the daily decision-making activities of both the private and public sectors.

Approaches to the implementation of land-use policies, planning, and programs at the regional level would best center around the information-coordination-technical assistance functions of these areawide agencies. Within such a three-part framework, the regional planning agency can effectively initiate and develop land-use planning techniques. Information can be disseminated to local governments and citizen groups on new federal and state enabling legislation, on new techniques in land-use planning, and on the role of land-use controls in their particular region. The coordination can occur where the regional agency brings together local government agencies, elected officials, and citizen groups to effectively inform them about new developments, new problems, and present activities in land-use planning. Technical assistance can occur where the regional agency designs and completes the actual zoning ordinance and/or land-use plans.

This array of functional activities can then be matched against three land-use planning objectives. The first would involve the development and adoption of a regional land-use plan, multi-county in scope, dealing with broad developmental growth trends and policies, closely related to the efforts of a state land-use planning system, and recognizing and reacting to any national land-use policies and programs. Secondly, the development of countywide land-use plans can serve the purpose of an official document for the county, delineate basic problems facing it, and offer specific land-use planning recommendations. Thirdly, land-use plans and their related legal tools may be reduced to a smaller scope involving planning area land-use plans, and perhaps where necessary to an even smaller scope that would involve a site-design land-use plan for a specific area.

As a result of this framework or any like procedure, the many complex land-use issues that face Appalachia can be dealt with in such a way that the ultimate goal will be to achieve concrete and tangible results. Many of the prevailing issues of land use in Appalachia, such as growth or no-growth, the spatial arrangement of socioeconomic activities, and environmental preservation or use can be approached in a positive and constructive way. More specifically, these issues reflect the hard choices needed for the development of land for industry, commerce, and residential use (a "growth is good" philosophy) versus controlled population and socioeconomic growth; the arrangement of these activities in designed patterns versus uncontrolled and unregulated growth; the effect on the natural environment of Appalachia of the extractive nature of some economic activities.

In short, land-use planning in Appalachia cannot be simply a reiteration of "critical issues" facing the region. These issues, which have time and time again been published, stated, and restated, must be placed in a mechanism that can operate in a constructive fashion. It is time for positions and policies to be carried out through whatever means we have at our disposal. For, without a concerted effort in applying these policies in our day-to-day decision-making routine, they become nothing more than the overblown rhetoric with which we are all too familiar.

Jack S. Kelley
USDA Forest Service
National Forests in North Carolina
P.O. Box 2750, Asheville, N.C. 28802

Most forest land in the Appalachians is in private ownership, usually of small acreage. These forest lands are not being managed on sound land-use principles, but on the policy of short-term economic gain rather than long-term management of their natural resources.

Most states and local governments throughout the Appalachian Mountains do not have land-use regulations. State Forestry departments assist small landowners in marketing their timber and using wise land-use procedures to insure future crops of timber, but the service is not regulated and is only provided to those who request it.

Presently much forested land is being developed for resorts, summer-home sites, and other uses, resulting in overdevelopment of marginal sites. The question isn't so much whether or not a summer home should be built on a mountain top, but whether the natural resources, mainly the soil, will support such a structure. Also, will the soil properly handle sewage disposal, et cetera?

Large landowners and public land-managing agencies such as the U.S. Forest Service have long-range planning processes to insure the perpetuation of natural resources. In timber management, this is called sustained-yield management.

The National Forests within the Southern and Central Appalachians contain 5 million acres. They are the Monongahela, Pisgah, Nantahala, Cherokee, George Washington, Jefferson, Chattahoochee, and part of the Sumter.

Management decisions in this area integrate the needs of people--both attractive surroundings and opportunities for gainful employment, with effective management of the natural resources.

The Appalachian hardwood ecosystem is a basic unit of nature comprising both organisms and their environment, interacting with each other. Multiple-use planning begins with an understanding of this ecosystem and its interactions, for together with social and economic considerations, it provides a basis for coordinated regional land-use planning and management. Management within the ecosystem considers the needs of all species of plants and animals as well as what it can produce.

In harvesting timber, product considerations are made for wildlife, stream protection, and effective recreation opportunities. Harvest methods are regeneration and intermediate thinnings. Regeneration cuts are accomplished by either seed tree, shelterwood, or clearcut methods. Intermediate cutting is by either non-commercial or commercial thinnings.

In 1973 on National Forest land in the Appalachians of North Carolina, silvicultural work consisted of planting or seeding over 3,000 acres; natural regeneration established about the same acreage. Thinning has been accomplished on nearly 2,500 acres. A 250-acre seed orchard is in operation to produce seed for superior trees.

Virgin stands of timber are scattered throughout Appalachia but only a few are of any size, namely Joyce Kilmer Memorial Forest in North Carolina with 3,800 acres, Linville Gorge with 7,600 acres, and Ramseys Draft in Virginia with 1,800 acres.

Third Session: THE HUMAN SPIRIT

After introductions by Borden Mace, of the Appalachian Consortium, Reverend R. Baldwin Lloyd, of the Appalachian Peoples' Service Organization, led off the group session with his feelings on the human spirit, especially as shown in the mountain regions. Fundamentally he felt that its strength lies in knowing oneself and one's brother and sister, in understanding them in relation to community life, and in living in harmony with the creative forces of life. If God gives man dominion over the birds, beasts, and fishes, it is only so that he may share and care for and love His creation. To use and to be in harmony with creation are a blessing; to abuse it is a curse that leads to loss of the human spirit. As demonstrated in Appalachia, the men who have become corporate men have lost sight of this spirit in the poor and thereby in themselves. Mr. Lloyd observed with regret the absence at the conference of representatives of the miners and the poor. Mr. Mace replied that, although many had been invited, few had been able to attend.

Novelist and historian Wilma Dykeman Stokely followed with a conversation on the human spirit as it has been eroded but survives in the region. Regarding the prevalence of misery and exploitation, her overall observation was that the past is never past--past problems unmet, compounded by apathy and neglect, are still present problems. Beneath this visible misery, however, still lies the real Appalachian character, with its strength, independence, and integrity. She illustrated this with extensive and appropriate passages from her books.[1,2,3,4]

By the nature of the subject, the small-group sessions were unable to arrive at a definition of the human spirit, not so much because it is vague as because it is so complex. The outcome of these concurrent sessions was therefore fragmentary, not conclusive. Among the observations were that:

1. while material comforts can frequently dull man's spirit, they can also relieve him from hunger, drudgery, and disease
2. the wants and needs of the nation must be weighed against its spiritual choices
3. the colonial, urban viewpoint dulls the native, rural values
4. appropriate energy use can give man leisure for spiritual and intellectual contemplation

---

[1] Wilma Dykeman Stokely. *Tall Woman*. New York: Holt, Rinehart & Winston, 1962.

[2] _____ *The French Broad*. Knoxville: University of Tennessee Press, 1966.

[3] _____ *Look to This Day*. New York: Holt, Rinehart & Winston, 1968.

[4] _____ *The Far Family*. New York: Avon, 1972.

5. Appalachian independence is vanishing under the influx of outsiders (students, tourists, second-homers), some of whom are semi-permanent, some transient
6. even when mountain folk go away to work, their regional spirit survives
7. certain unique qualities of the Appalachians (language, dialect, music, crafts, dancing) may affect their acceptance or rejection by the outside world
8. on occasion, we blame not the exploiter, but the exploited--for being ignorant, for selling his birthright for little return
9. not all regions of Appalachia are alike in want or need, e.g., Kentucky and Georgia
10. the effects of absentee ownership have been generally disastrous when compared with the small but immediate benefits of income, education, and health services
11. a frustration by givers and receivers alike is determining where help ends and interference begins
12. some regional values, both spiritual and material, must change to meet the future
13. local action must establish the limits of cooperation vs. competition
14. both the cultural universals and the folk insights should be preserved; outside agencies are likely to destroy, rather than encourage, unique traits; options, not directions, should be given

15. aspirations should not be raised without the means to achieve them
16. the attitudes of the change agents should perhaps be changed, rather than the mountaineers' outlook
17. mountain crafts should be promoted as a form of creativity, not for their quaintness
18. Appalachian resources are needed nationally and worldwide, but the region <u>must</u> receive its fair share
19. corporations have been maximizing their profits; it is now time for Appalachians to maximize the quality of their daily lives
20. remnants of a belief in white magic and the benign practices of witchcraft have given mountain people a sustaining harmony with their surroundings and the spirit of God and man
21. the spirit, insofar as it implies transcendence, freedom, and creativity is destined for destruction in Orwell's <u>1984</u>; the manifestation of the Appalachian spirit refuses to be intimidated by this prospect of a dehumanizing technology
22. the gross exploitation of Central Appalachia's natural wealth is having a dire and direct effect on the spirit of its inhabitants, for it is eroding their trust in their fellow men and their government
23. the spirit of Appalachia is well demonstrated in the spirit of the freedom-loving loners who sought out and settled in the mountains to keep their independence and self-reliance

24. the distinctive culture of Appalachia is threatened both by the corporate exploiters and by the intrusive do-gooders
25. the Appalachian inherited a sturdy, self-reliant, stoic, reserved, and gentle way of life; it is in danger of extinction through loss of family cohesiveness even though material progress has brought improvements in health care, job openings, education, and housing
26. whether the mountain spirit can challenge, where necessary, and adapt to, where appropriate, the outside forces in control of so much of their resources must be faced
27. if urbanization and technology cannot be contained, their advance may mean the inevitable destruction of Appalachian spirit and culture
28. education should enable the mountain folk to communicate their special spirit, not replace it with new values
29. if the human spirit, Appalachian or otherwise, is truly transcendent, the future is open, not predetermined, unchangeable, or mechanistic
30. how best can the regional spirit survive the assaults of industry and a mainstream society whose temptations may rob and deplete it?

From this rich array of observations, both hopeful and fearful, the reader will no doubt absorb the same feeling of frustration as many of the participants--a definition of the Human Spirit never emerged. The question of its nurture, however, was no problem--it can be fed in many ways as long as the diet is rich in love, compassion, and respect for a man's dignity.

THE HUMAN SPIRIT

Helen Matthews-Lewis
Clinch Valley College
University of Virginia
Wise, Virginia 24293

Appalachia has a long history of struggle for survival in a long history of exploitation. Strip mining, tourist development, and industries seeking cheap labor are just recent chapters. It is an area incredibly rich in natural resources. Descriptions of it when early explorers came tell of the bounty of land and forest.

The first exploitation was probably the game. Then the wealth of timber was discovered and the lumbering industry unmercifully cut away one of the finest forests of the world's temperate zone. The discovery of coal by geologists, industrialists, and New York and British financiers was the next documented take-over. Coal mining has since removed billions of tons of coal with little return to the area. Strip mining, dams, and ski resorts may be the death blows, but they are only insult added to years of injury. Those who once lived off the land and forest have become timberers, coal miners, cheap labor for factories, and economic refugees in the city.

But mountain people have resisted and survived, and some mountain culture has been preserved through the families and the mountain churches despite the massive invasion of outside colonizers and civilizers who developed "brought-on" churches, schools, and other social institutions inimical to mountain ways. Their failures have been a testimony to the strength and persistence of an integrated culture.

The traditional mountain way of life is antagonistic to urban, industrial, class-structured ways and values. It is more egalitarian and cooperative. Based on hunting and subsistence agriculture, it developed a way of life that stressed both independence and mutual aid. People should be self-sufficient and not <u>depend</u> on others for help, but if they can, they should be accommodating and help their neighbor. This mutual aid operates from a position of equality, a way of life that is antagonistic to situations of inequality, elitism, or hierarchical organization.

Early visitors remarked on the friendly, equal relationships, on how generous and uncompetitive the mountain people were. Today, teachers find mountain students lacking achievement motivation, cooperative in play, and avoiding conflict. Mountain people were said to be free from self-consciousness, direct, open, dignified, and courteous. It was not a cold, staid culture, but an expressive one with rhythm, eloquence, and great emotion shown in speech, song, theology, and religious expression.

The destructive process still goes on and, although it is more dramatic where strip mining now occurs, it is happening throughout the mountains. Land, timber, natural beauty for recreation, and cheap labor are still sought and secured in Appalachia.

With strip mining, we see more dramatically the dwelling places of mountain people destroyed and damaged. Strip mining also destroys a way of life and a way of looking at life. Strip miners treat mountains as just another commodity to develop or exploit, while mountain people have traditionally been less manipulative, more adaptive to the physical environment.

Strip mining with its callous destruction results from a way of life based on competition, drive for profit, and a belief in the superiority of a technological world. As we destroy and sacrifice Appalachia for the energy needs of the country, we are destroying a culture more humane, more in balance with nature, and more concerned with a good life than with a good living.

J.P. Lucas, Jr., Vice President, Public Affairs
Duke Power Company
Charlotte, North Carolina 28201

For years the Appalachia of the sociologists has been the native heath of a clannish and homespun folk given to small arts and crafts, folk-dancing, and the operation of countless illegal stills, all in a setting of hardship, if not grim despair. But the influx of outside support, the strengthening of education, new medical and other social services, the advent of substantial industry, and the incredible land boom have changed a way of life.

The risk is that in this rapid change mountain men and women may lose some of the human values that made them a unique segment of American society. The qualities of directness and candor, of fortitude and faith, and of independence of spirit can gradually erode in a new-found prosperity. Many social problems still press in upon people, and opportunity is needed for the application of new knowledge and for the employment of many skills by a new generation of mountain folk.

A people may choose to be farmers, factory workers, teachers, technicians, or real estate agents--but <u>citizens</u> they must be, citizens with as much as education can give them of personal integrity, community responsibility, and spiritual awareness.

With so much emphasis on things that society does for the deprived individual, it is important to distinguish between social security and personal security, which proceeds only from what the individual does for himself. Encouraging people to believe in their own helplessness holds the seeds of tragedy. This is worth thinking about as a regional group as we face new dimensions of living in a new and perilous world. Our sense of national purpose must arise out of voluntary thought and action, and must represent the sum of the convictions, ideals, intelligence, and deepest desires of the people.

Unless our primary goal is to be a great <u>people</u> we cannot for long expect to be a great <u>nation</u>. As a nation, we need a leavening of the pioneer tradition and a way of life that is more than the pursuit of money. The time has come when men may look less to Washington and more to their native hills.

American Petroleum Institute
1801 K Street, N.W.
Washington, D.C. 20006

The American Petroleum Institute claims no particular expertise in the human spirit. We would like to point out, however, that the availability of energy has been a powerful factor in human development and profoundly affects the human spirit.

The United States is blessed by energy abundance. In the age when wood was the major energy source, our forefathers came to a continent covered with forests. When the age of coal arrived, we found that areas such as Appalachia contained what then seemed to be inexhaustible reserves. When oil became a major energy source, it seemed that our Southwestern states were floating on oil.

The correlation between energy consumption and living standards is extremely close. Nations with high living standards have high per-capita energy consumption; those with low living standards are associated with low energy consumption. Some people in Appalachia still rely upon wood and on human and animal power for energy. All too often, these are in places of hardship, poverty, and despair that crush the human spirit and destroy human initiative.

Human progress involves more than the mere acquisition of material goods. A human being is not necessarily better off if he has an electric blanket instead of a regular blanket. Such items are not necessarily uplifting to the human spirit, but some aspects of higher living standards do have value. For example, people with higher living standards can eat more nutritious foods, are healthier, and usually live longer. They can afford proper medical and dental treatment. Health affects human attitudes and the enjoyment of a full life.

Another benefit of the higher living standards associated with energy consumption is increased leisure. No longer does man have to work from sunup to sundown just to provide food and clothing for himself and his family. He has time to get an education, to learn more about the planet on which he lives, and to enjoy art, music, or literature. These things act to expand man's horizons and uplift his spirit.

Mankind has not yet learned to make full use of the benefits of being freed from devoting all his energies to obtaining the basic necessities of life. He is still beset by constant fruitless wars, by the increasing population, by a too-hectic pace of life, and by increasing violence and crime. These problems will not be solved by a return to the hardships and misery associated with low energy consumption.

In our nation, energy has always been cheap and abundant and, as to be expected, it has often been wasted--a waste we can no longer afford. Wise use of energy can contribute to the advancement of the human spirit, to human progress, and to man's general expansion and development. Decisions on how it will be used must be made by all members of society.

Tennessee Valley Authority
Knoxville, Tennessee 37902

One day in 1907, as Gifford Pinchot, chief forester under President Theodore Roosevelt, rode through the park, he was struck by a new concept:

> The forest and its relation to streams and inland navigation, to water power and flood control, to the soil and its erosion, to coal and oil and other resources--these questions would not let [me] be. . . .
> Suddenly the idea flashed through my head that there was a unity in this complication--that the relation of one resource to another was not the end of the story. . . . Seen in this new light, all these separate questions fitted into and made up one great central problem of the use of the earth for the good of man.

Pinchot might have added that the proper use of resources, recognizing this interrelationship, opens the door for the human spirit. Tennessee Valley farmers of the 1930s depleted the soils, fostered erosion, and led impoverished lives. Drudgery was the burial ground of human energy--and the human spirit.

Pinchot's philosophy, as embodied in the Tennessee Valley Authority, wrought great changes in this way of life. Farmers learned to use fertilizers, to heal their gullies, to plant pastures, and to shift to animal agriculture. Electricity brought labor-saving devices to the farm wife throughout the valley. New industries opened opportunities for skillful hands and alert minds. The horizons of the human spirit were greatly expanded.

Today, the character of economic growth and social change in the Tennessee Valley has given a unique cast to many of the problems faced by the area.

SOLID WASTE. An expanding population demands more products, many of which eventually wind up on the trash heaps. TVA helped in this field when it saw that many communities lacked the technical know-how for locating and designing landfills and enough private engineering consultants to do the job. Its success is best illustrated by the junk car collection program. More than 25,000 junked and abandoned automobiles have been collected and recycled since the program began in the latter part of 1970.

AVOIDING FLOOD DAMAGES. One persistent problem of any community is the management of its waters. Twenty years ago, TVA undertook a program of working with the people to avoid flood damage where floods could not be prevented--to "keep the people away from the water where you can't keep the water away from the people." On local request and with state participation, TVA flood control engineers analyze the flood problems of a community. More than 130 communities have taken advantage of this program.

MAKING NEW TOWNS OUT OF OLD. Many small- and medium-sized towns were built in another era and are unequipped to serve the new industry, commerce, and tourism in the region. TVA's program in this field, called "Townlift," is designed to unite both public and private sectors in defining and seizing the opportunities available.

HEALTH SERVICES IN RURAL AREAS. One of the most needed services in rural areas, and the most difficult to provide, is adequate health care. TVA has a number of sophisticated tools, acquired for its own use, which it is now using in cooperation with public and private medical organizations in the region. We hope that locally managed programs will evolve.

EDUCATION. TVA's concern is directed in part to providing technical and financial assistance to public school systems, higher education, and any other segment of public education.

RURAL FIRE PROTECTION. For a combination of reasons, tragically understandable and explainable, rural fire protection has been a neglected field of community action. TVA in 1973 made arrangements for a pilot project that revives the old-fashioned volunteer fire department principle dressed up with modern technology. For example, volunteers are summoned to an emergency by an electronic paging system using pocket-sized portable radio receivers.

Man's ability to use his opportunities and solve his problems will always be limited. These examples, however, show TVA's pragmatic approach to working with the people of the region to remove some of the limitations and to encourage individual initiative.

Louis H. Hunter, Executive Vice President
National Independent Coal Operators' Association
Richlands, Virginia 24641

Various concepts of the human spirit have been put forward by many individuals at different times in history. Let us develop the concept of the human spirit as a good steward. To do this, we must assume that the earth is the Lord's: "the world and they that dwell therein" (Ps. 24:1). All resources of the earth belong to God. Their use by the human spirit must at all times be governed by God's laws and guided by His purposes. The human spirit is then entrusted with the care and use of the earth and its resources. Private ownership of the earth is man-made and under the supervision of the human spirit. I believe that it is God's will that the resources of the earth be developed, conserved, and used in ways that bring maximum benefit, fulfillment, and abundance of life to all persons.

Some advocate a ban on the use of resources and the land, but how could a human be a good steward if his life were lived out in doing nothing to help other people, understand who they are, why they are here, where they came from, and where they will go once this life is over?

The human spirit as a good steward involves every area of life on this planet and is the investment of time, talents, energy, and abilities in the land and its resources.

Pocahontas Land Corporation
Bluefield, West Virginia

Many visitors have tried to describe the human spirit of Appalachia and its people, but their accounts have failed to broaden an understanding of this spirit and have left the impression that the Appalachian people are a cold, close-knit breed who lack an interest in the outside world and live only with a hope that things will get better tomorrow. A native of the area finds all their views wanting. The people of Appalachia are a warm, generous people, who know and understand hard work and share everyone's desire for a better way of life.

Appalachia is not without its problems, but through the dedication and inspiration of many individuals, corporations, foundations, and the federal, state, and local governments, the lives of the residents are improving. The efforts of Appalachian residents to lift themselves are exemplified by periodic stories of work on civic and regional improvements. The success stories include the development of the Appalachian Trail, the Blue Ridge Parkway, the Great Smoky Mountains National Park, numerous schools and community colleges, and Gatlinburg, Tennessee.

It should be remembered that, in each of those successful efforts, citizens understood the common objective and worked hard to achieve it, whether the effort was directed toward developing the Appalachian Trail, which traverses the entire region, or toward building an outdoor theatre for local events, as many cities and towns have done. While it is hard to define the human spirit of Appalachia and its residents, it is this spirit that tells the mountaineer he would like to have just one person--one day--come into his hollow and show some signs of approval--not try to change him without first attempting to know and understand him.

LENOWISCO* Planning District Commission
Duffield, Virginia 24244

We have a situation in America, and more recently in Appalachia, where the human spirit is no longer being glorified, but is in danger of being irrevocably damaged. The thrust of the American Democracy of 1776 was to place on the individual the burden of responsibility for his own life and for that of his country. In two hundred years, amid excuses of too many people, efficiency, and equality, this process has been almost completely reversed and many question whether we even have democracy. We have a situation in which we commonly refer to our elected officials as being "at the top" and the people "at the bottom." This terminology alone indicates that something is badly wrong.

Some contend that only a revolution will reverse our direction, but there are more peaceful ways of dealing with this problem. Mid-Appalachia, being outside the mainstream of American life for so many years, has not been quite so affected. Consequently, we are what many refer to as a "stubborn breed." Appalachia is still rife with people who retain that native American spirit, who want to make their own decisions and be responsible for their own lives. It is the ideal place to begin to reverse what is happening in America. Contrary to the professed beliefs of the decision makers, people are capable of making the choices necessary to govern their own lives

Agencies involved in making decisions must start to make a real effort to involve the people they serve in the entire process. Regional planning agencies can and should play a major role in this transition. Much of

---

*The Cities of Lee, Norton, Wise, and Scott, Virginia.

the work of these agencies can profoundly affect the lives of the people they serve, and the people are rarely, if ever, directly involved in the planning. Admittedly, trying to involve a large number of people in decision making will require more energy than we are used to expending, but someone must start.

W. Grady Stumbo, M.D., President
East Kentucky Health Services Center, Inc.
Hindman, Kentucky 41882

Almost 60 years ago, Horace Kephart wrote that "the mountaineers of today are face to face with a mighty change . . . the mountaineer at last is to be caught up in the current of human progress." Nothing so dramatic happened, and again today, the Appalachian region has been rediscovered by more people and more programs than any of us can remember.

Appalachia is a complex geographical and cultural society. One can describe the Appalachian as a proud backwoodsman of English ancestry who pays his own way in a life isolated from the rest of the world. One can also describe him as a ne'er-do-well, living off handouts, and wanting to be classified as totally and permanently disabled. Both descriptions are true, over-simplified, and prejudicial. Any attempt to stereotype him leads to incorrect assumptions.

Huge agencies organized for the Appalachians' interest, with bureaucratic precision, generate band-aid remedies that are sold as concrete efforts at problem solving, but they signify only betrayed hopes and broken promises. The "do-gooders" have defined them not responsible and attempt to impose paternalism, a concept rapidly being rejected by Appalachian residents. They are becoming so organized that expanded programs within the area have begun to give new life to the region.

Among perpendicular hills, people still live in hollows, some of which are isolated from the population centers in the area. The economic growth centers are booming and are developing many characteristics generally found in this country. Their development has resulted in a sharp separation of "the haves" and "the have nots." We have been told that the people who live in the hollows must move to the centers as defined by the government. The hollows must be flooded to serve as electrical and water resources for the rest of the country. The development of these "economic growth centers" now makes it possible for the hillbilly to become a migrant in his own land--in the move from the hollow to the county-seat town.

Among bureaucrats, co-ordination is a dirty word. Each agency goes about its work in the hollows with nothing but contempt for the others.

As justification for such actions, one is told how badly the Appalachian measures up against the rest of the nation--how far behind he is in infant mortality, educational opportunities, and social activities. Resident hillbillies have never had much say in such decisions, but today the number of young Appalachian leaders is growing; they do not buy such cultural destruction. They have become educated, they have seen the mistakes, and still they have maintained the ability to relate to the resident hillbilly.

One program is called the East Kentucky Health Services Center, a family-centered, primary-care facility offering a wide range of services reaching out from a professionally staffed ambulatory care center into the community with programs of preventive medicine. Primary care is delivered in the clinic by a team of physicians, nurses, community health advocates, and para-medical support personnel. The outreach efforts involve all staff members. EKHSC brought into the area the first laboratory, the first X-ray facilities, the first round-the-clock emergency coverage, a sliding fee-for-service practice, and many other innovations.

It is in this kind of effort, where the changes are initiated by outsiders but governed by mountaineers, that the future lies. Here the doors of isolation can be opened, not in one sudden leap, but gradually, thus retaining what is good about the mountain way of living.

Richard C. Jackson
Lees-McRae College
Banner Elk, North Carolina

The following viewpoint may fairly represent that of some people who have neither aligned themselves with any group nor formed their own.

I believe that a person has the right to do as he sees fit with his talents, gifts, land, and money, but it would be wrong for me (alone or with others) to force another person to do what seemed right to me. It is wrong to attempt to coerce another to use his resources in a certain way. It is also immoral to use one's talents and resources without regard for the welfare and dignity of one's neighbors, for the needs of those who will come after, or for the well-being of the earth itself.

Enough attempts have been made to push people into "right" decisions, with more than enough disregard for neighbors, posterity, and the earth. It doesn't matter a great deal if we call it zoning, land-use planning, development, or just progress. Zoning, land-use planning, development, and progress are not in themselves undesirable, but the ways we have gone about initiating them are subject to question. The particular danger lies in our tendency to claim goodness for what is not good and to base decisions on inaccurate premises.

Entertainment, recreation, rest, quietness, and prosperity are all seen as good. Consequently, the means to these ends (promotion of tourism, second homes, resorts, etc.) are also regarded as good. We have not inquired much into how things have been accomplished, what the long-range costs are, who benefits most, or what are the implications of the kinds of recreation that have been promoted. Until we have examined these matters closely, we stand in danger of having accepted, and acclaimed, a kind of cheap progress that ignores some basic human concerns: Is health care better? Is there less crime? Has the judicial process improved? Has alcoholism declined? Do the aged have more options?

Many manifestations are disturbing. The "mountain way" is touted as being quiet and restful, but a lot of the paraphernalia of urban regions is being brought in to support a growing population of people accustomed to "conveniences." In short, the qualities that attracted people in the first place are rapidly being eroded. I believe that community, an important concept, is endangered. I cannot understand the "community" that stations guards at the entrances or is composed primarily of absentees who leave their driveways blocked by chains and gates.

Cratis D. Williams
Appalachian State University
Boone, North Carolina

Traditionally, the life of the Appalachian mountain man was self-contained, complete, harsh at times, frustrated by conflict occasionally, and marooned in isolation generally, but nevertheless a satisfying and challenging life in the midst of rolling hills where he pastured his livestock, followed his traditions as a hunter, found the timber for his skills with wood, and gathered medicinal herbs for his health needs. He was self-sufficient, independent, and fiercely proud.

In his isolation, he has kept alive those virtues and qualities of character that for his ancestors, at the time of the American Revolution, had been the strength that enabled 13 struggling colonies to resist successfully the tyranny of one of the powerful nations of the world. By remaining content with fewer material goods and fewer creature comforts, he increased his wealth of confidence, leisure, and accouterments of relaxation. He had more time to do what he wanted than men in the larger society had, and he knew how to enjoy time as it came to him.

The simplicity of life in the mountains and the rich texture of the traditions there have become the envy in recent years of a jaded and falling American middle class, that long-touted moral backbone of our civilization groping painfully for some sign of regeneration, for some hope of relief from the tax burden, from the pressures of a society in which even the production of food has been preempted by big business, from the disruptions of every-day processes by greedy self-seekers, from the decay of the cities, from the paving of the countryside, and from the pollution of the atmosphere and the water sources.

Just when Americans look with longing toward the mountains, the mountains themselves, so long symbols of freedom and independence, have been preempted by the ruthless bulldozers that lay hopeless waste to the highlands themselves.

To cultivate again the dormant culture of the mountains, to provide more room for the human being himself to function as a free individual, we must preserve the mountains and save Appalachia from becoming a wasteland.

Conclusion

In these days of endless (and frequently futile) conferences, the Southern Appalachian Regional Conference, in its earnestness and enthusiasm, was an example to all. Its main topics--Energy, Land Use, The Human Spirit--while convenient for starting points for discussion, turned out to be inseparable.

The worldwide need for ENERGY makes Appalachia a prime target of both the needy and the greedy. The mineowners use a legitimate resource, but leave little profit with the original owners; skim off the easily stripped areas, leaving rich veins virtually inaccessible; and abandon the land, frequently beyond reclamation. The owners generally avoid the deep though richer mines because of higher wages to the workers and because of a growing insistence that they abide by costly health and safety regulations. This ravage of the land has side effects less immediately visible--the building of otherwise useless roads, the harm to existing roads by heavy trucks and other machinery, and leaving the denuded land open to erosion and flooding.

All the energy acquisition and use are, of course, a major, if not _the_ major, aspect of LAND USE in Appalachia. Other problems affecting the land are the preservation of food acreage in a world approaching subsistence reserves (if not starvation), the matter of cutting timber for lumber or pulp weighed against letting it stand for flood control and water supply, the opening of the wilderness beauty for the delight of all vs. its destruction by those whom it was meant to please.

Appalachian energy resources and land use both affect the HUMAN SPIRIT of the region. Where is the limit for any of the following?

1. extracting the coal for genuine need
2. applying the profits to local individuals and communities
3. opening the scenic areas to outsiders
4. preserving the timber, the agriculture land, and the water resources
5. the distribution of the economic benefits of both land use and coal mining to the original owners in their fight against ignorance, drudgery, and disease.

It can thus be seen that each benefit must be weighed against a possible harm. The participants in this conference have done exactly that, as the following statement by the Goals and Objectives Committee and a dissenting opinion from another group will show.

Statement
by
The Goals and Objectives Committee
SOUTHERN APPALACHIAN REGIONAL CONFERENCE
BOONE, NORTH CAROLINA
May 16, 1974

The following statement was derived from a careful consideration of the major suggestions, concerns, and objectives put forth during the concurrent sessions of the conference.

Recognizing that the patience of the people in Appalachia has been strained for many years, recognizing that past practices of the extractive and other industries have imposed not only great injustices, but also social and private costs upon the people, anticipating further a major increase in coal production for the immediate future, we urge the consideration of the following* observations, objectives, and concerns:

1. Since change is inevitable in Appalachia, and long-range planning for the quality of life in the region is desirable, it must include a concern for traditional values and cannot be done without the people shaping their own destiny.

2. The people of Appalachia must therefore become more active in the decisions that affect their future. Of particular significance are the decisions affecting educational institutions, land use policy, and economic development. Many important decisions about the future of the region must come from local communities; the people therefore urgently need to develop a sense of self-determination and a more sensitized, equitable, and responsive mountain leadership.

---

*The sequence of items is no indication of their priority.

3. Educational institutions in Appalachia must relate more consciously to the mountain experience. They must include a concern for the rich historical and cultural heritage of the region, an awareness of the relationship between human beings and their land, and of the alternatives for the future and for the human values involved.

As for land-use planning, the following objectives are of major importance. Planners must:

1. develop through education the understanding by decision makers and by the general public of the physical, human, and economic impact and consequences of their decisions and of the effective use of the planning process as a tool for making their decisions and actions produce the maximum benefits to individuals and society. (Decisions might result in no change as well as controlled change.)

2. obtain the recognition at local, state, and national levels that the mountain terrain is a sensitive environment of limited capacity for development. It is essential to realize that the <u>lack</u> of rational, informed guidance and control of land use can generate crisis conditions in which subsequent recovery costs are excessive and the opportunity to protect and preserve basic values may be foreclosed

3. accumulate a considerably improved data base for the region, for sub-regions, and for localities so that land-use decisions can be

supported factually, and develop the methodology to facilitate the use of this information for decision making

4. establish local implementation and enforcement of land-use controls that are locally determined instead of using the minimum standards and guidelines established at state and federal levels; the acceptance of state and federal guidelines is still necessary because land use and its changes affect areas beyond local political boundaries

5. establish patterns of land use that favor clustering over widespread dispersal wherever it can be shown that the environmental and social impact can thereby be minimized

6. provide for the development at local levels of land-use policies that reflect local values and the development capacity of the region. The relative long-term effects of growth versus no-growth policies should be critically examined

7. establish and maintain as basic the right of all individuals potentially affected by land-use changes to be heard through public hearings and petition

8. establish as a responsibility of those who cause change to provide all pertinent information that will allow for a comprehensive evaluation of the on-site and off-site, short-term and long-term effects of the proposed change for purposes of approval. In addition, the principle of planned sequential use should be applied to all extractive industries to insure long-term community benefits as a consequence of their practices

9. devise feasible ways to reclaim areas that have suffered from inappropriate land use in the past
10. facilitate the use of experts in tax-supported colleges and universities as a public service available to the community to protect its interests and the interests of society in general.

In the area of energy supply and consumption we find the following observations vitally important. The goals of national energy policy ought to be _equity_ and _efficiency_. We therefore make the following specific recommendations:

1. The goals of energy conservation and the promotion of increased energy production can best be achieved by permitting the price mechanism to work. We recognize that at present certain barriers distort these market forces, namely:

    a. the lack of accurate information

    b. uncertainty

    c. market imperfections such as the ownership of the major fuel sources by the international petroleum cartels.

    Where the price mechanism causes special hardship to segments of the population or to certain workers or businesses, the inequities ought to be corrected, but distortion of the _basic_ market system ought not be used to achieve the corrections, e.g., where low-income families are adversely affected by higher fuel costs or where a changing fuel market brings about unemployment. A solution to the first hardship might be some form of income supplement; a possible solution to the second would be funds for retraining, for moving costs, or for easing the burden of sudden unemployment.

2. Prices and costs of each energy producer ought to reflect <u>full costs, including all social and private costs</u>, so as to prevent, as far as possible, harmful social and private costs. This could best be achieved by federal legislation, setting national standards in health and safety, environment, and reclamation. States should have the option of setting higher standards. In addition, for certain social and private costs (such as highway construction, welfare costs, and damage to property), only states and localities can and should provide remedies. It is understood that such legislation must be vigorously enforced.

3. Increased research and development to explore existing and alternative energy systems are needed. These systems must be examined in terms of extraction, transportation, conversion, and use. We need to study the technology, economy, and impact on the individual and society of these questions. It is important to look not only at individual components of energy systems, but also at their interrelation. For instance, coal is in direct competition with nuclear fuels, oil, and gas in electric power production. Thus technological or market changes in any of these fuels will have repercussions on the coal industry and thus on Appalachia.

The following members of the Goals and Objectives Committee participated in the drafting of this statement of objectives and take full responsibility for its content:

Donald F. Crickmer   John R. Moore
Ronald Eller   James Noel
James Hackett   F. Schmidt-Bleek, Chairman
Ernest E. Hendrix   Neil M. Walp
Mary D. Houska

MINORITY REPORT STATEMENT

We recommend that this conference adopt a proposal to extend the Appalachian mountains a stay of execution. By this we mean that, while we are struggling with solutions to land use and stripping, it is imperative that the destructive actions be stopped until a reasonable study and policy be implemented to satisfy the will of the inhabitants of the affected areas. As it is, we are losing around 25 acres of land for each hour we carry on this dialogue. We find it irresponsible to sit in a burning building while planning ways to put the fire out.

Frank Kilgore	Helen Matthews Lewis
Rick Kirby	Kenneth Murray
Frank Taylor	Jerry Williamson
John Tiller	Charlotte T. Ross
Catherine Tiller	Jane Cummins
Jack Wright	James Branscome
Robert Raymond	Steve Fisher
Burt Purrington	Peggy Rives
Rhoda Cerny	Beth Bingman
Kent Cave	Linda Johnson
Judy Cornett	Mary Ellen Griffith

Appendix A

Speech by Governor James E. Holshouser, Jr.
Regional Conference on the Future of Southern Appalachia
Conference Theme
Toward 1984: The Future of Appalachia?
13 May 1974

We're all here for this conference because we share an interest in this unique and special part of the world known as Appalachia, and because we all have a role in shaping its future.

This is a big region. Its potential is unlimited, and its problems are complex. No longer is Appalachia an isolated, remote place of beauty, but, because of its vast and essential resources, its future has become closely and critically meshed with the future of this country--and even the world.

That's why we are here . . . that's why this conference is taking place. We will have different opinions . . . our interests may seem to conflict, but all of us recognize that the future of Appalachia (and perhaps the future of all of us) demands that there be careful and thoughtful consideration, a free exchange of ideas and viewpoints, and sound and sober planning.

I grew up in these mountains, and I've watched them change. Right here in this county, I have seen many changes in just a few short years. We've seen a gradual influx of new industry, providing better incomes to many of our people.

We've seen this area develop into a major, year-round tourist and recreation resort. We've seen the impact of such attractions as "Horn in the West," "Tweetsie Railroad," Grandfather Mountain and the Land of Oz on our economy and our way of life.

We've seen mountainsides transformed into ski slopes, bringing thousands of visitors and part-time residents to share our winters with us. We've seen total communities grow up around these resorts, complete with golf courses, swimming pools, and tennis courts.

We've seen this campus grow from a small teachers' college to a major state university, producing leaders and scholars in many fields, while Western Carolina University and the University of North Carolina at Asheville have made great strides. We've seen community colleges and technical institutes spring up throughout the mountains, bringing greater opportunities to our people.

None of these things could have happened without roads--the roads that have made these former "lost provinces" readily accessible to the world outside. In recent years, we have seen dramatic improvements in the highway systems serving all parts of Appalachia and have seen many airports constructed in the region.

The most important single force for these changes and economic improvements in this region has been the Appalachian Regional Commission (ARC). When the Appalachian Regional Development Act was passed in 1965, the 13-state Appalachian area had one of the largest concentrations of rural poverty in America. Unemployment was high, health services were sorely inadequate, and transportation systems were poor at best.

This program began as one of our nation's first large-scale experiments in state-federal partnership. The success of this partnership has been a major factor in the emergence of the so-called "New Federalism" that has reversed the flow of power to Washington and is starting to send it back to state and local governments.

Over the past eight years, Congress has pumped some $2.2 billion into this region through the Appalachian Regional Commission. In the 13-state area, it has spent $1.3 billion for highways, $258 million for health programs, $169 million for vocational education, $9.5 million for housing, and $330 million in supplemental grants for various public works projects.

In North Carolina alone, the ARC has provided more than $115 million to the 29 counties that are part of the Appalachian Region. This total includes more than $54 million for development of highways, almost $4 million for local access roads, $5 million for child development programs, $17 million for health programs, $1.5 million for soil conservation, $77,000 for timber development, almost $1 million for housing, $9.7 million for vocational education, almost $3 million for research, and $19 million to supplement other federal grants for construction of water systems, sewer systems, libraries, hospitals, industrial parks, solid waste systems, and other facilities.

The Appalachian Regional program has played a vital role in improving the quality of life for our people. State and local officials, and private business and industry have made great contributions to this goal. This is not to say that the job is done, or even that we're approaching the finish line, but we have made progress.

Yet progress, too, has its hazards. If we rush pell-mell to develop these mountainsides, to harness the rivers, and to remove the mineral resources, without looking to either side to see what is happening, we could wake up one day and find ourselves wondering if this is the same land that we all knew and loved.

We know that this region--possibly more than any other--offers our best hope for solution of the country's energy problems and for enabling the United States to meet its energy needs independent of other countries.

We know that the coal is there, but we also know the environmental dangers involved. It's a big job, but one we can do.

America has met so many challenges . . . the challenge of landing on the moon . . . the challenge of finding a vaccine for polio. Who is going to say that we cannot lick this challenge? With careful determination, we can find a way to remove the tremendous reservoir of coal that remains in the ground without doing irreparable damage to the mountains.

In this, however, as in all we do, we must plan and work to make sure that we protect ourselves, that we don't wake up to find someday that we have let slip all the good things these mountains mean to us.

An elusive term known as "quality of life" includes the ability of a man to provide for himself and his family, but it encompasses more than that--more than income or bricks and mortar. It also encompasses our environment--the air we breathe, the water we drink, and the beauty of the earth and trees and flowers.

That's what this conference is all about--Energy, Environment, and the Human Spirit.

I talked about growing up here in this corner of Appalachia, I talked about the changes I've seen, but I didn't mention the things that haven't changed, the intangibles that had an even greater impact on me.

I'm talking about the great human and moral values that are ingrained in our people--values such as thrift, paying our own way, knowing that, with most people, a man's word is as good as his bond.

These values are a vital part of Appalachia--perhaps the best part. As we look to the future of Appalachia, let us not neglect the importance of preserving these values and sharing them with the rest of the world.

Appendix B

John B. Howard
Development of Energy Resources
An Address to the
Southern Appalachian Regional Conference
Boone, North Carolina
13 May 1974

I was asked to come down to speak on one of the three topics of this conference--energy. In a sense, the entire conference is on energy. Since all but a small fraction of the energy we use comes from the land, land use and energy are inseparable. Energy also has a powerful impact on the human being--since lack of energy can mean poverty and despair and a dampening of the human spirit.

It is a pleasure for me to return to Appalachia. I say "return" because I was a reporter for U.S. News and World Report for a decade. This was the decade of Lyndon B. Johnson's war on poverty, and much attention was directed toward Appalachia.

When we realized Appalachia was to be in the news, we decided to find someone who understood the region. I was impressed by a book entitled "Night Comes to the Cumberlands," written by Harry Caudill (whom some of you may know) and decided to go to Whitesburg, Kentucky to interview him. Following that interview, we got in his car for a tour of Appalachia I will never forget. We drove up the "hollers," over roads that were indescribable; I saw poverty such as I had not seen in our big cities. I met people to whom welfare was a way of life. I saw, long before environment became a cause in this country, the results of environmental negligence. Mountains had been literally ripped apart, streams poisoned by acid, places of great scenic beauty destroyed. The impact on my thinking was lasting. I returned twice to write stories on the progress, or lack of progress, of government programs to help Appalachia. If at any time in the rest of my speech I sound like an anti-environmentalist, believe me I am not. Even if we have to crawl on our hands and knees from one town to the other for lack of energy, we cannot rape our land and destroy it for future generations.

Right off, of course, I am in deep trouble. You show great courage in asking someone from the oil industry to speak on energy here in coal country, but maybe it is appropriate after all. People working in the energy field recognize that they must look at the total energy picture--not just at one particular fuel. In recent years, we have seen dramatic demonstrations of the interrelationships between energy sources. What happens in one energy field can have a heavy impact on all others.

When you get right down to it, why do we have an energy problem? It is because coal can no longer be used in many of its major markets, because nuclear power has come on-stream much more slowly than anticipated, and because little additional energy has been available from hydropower. This means that petroleum--oil and natural gas--have had to bear a disproportionate share of the sharply increasing energy demand. Inadequate development of domestic petroleum resources made it necessary to turn to foreign oil to make up the energy shortfall. Then came the Arab oil embargo, and we discovered the folly of this policy.

The events of the past winter, grim as they were, probably had some beneficial effects. For one thing, we were reminded that our society is sewn together with the thread of energy. We had been told, ad nauseum, that the United States, with only 6% of the world's population, consumes over 30% of its energy. This fact was supposed to fill us with horror because of its supposed inequity. It is true, of course, that this country has wasted energy. Resources that are cheap and abundant are usually wasted, but if a nation had 30% of the world's population and 6% of its energy consumption, it would contain a poverty-stricken people slaving from sunup to sundown to try to feed and clothe themselves and their families.

Energy availability determines life styles. In the last century, the availability of coal, especially along our Eastern seaboard, transformed our nation from an agricultural to an industrial society. In this century, the gasoline-powered internal combustion engine has had equally far-reaching effects upon our lives. Just since World War II, we have seen a steadily increasing concentration of population in our large metropolitan areas and a huge expansion of suburbia made possible by the automobile. An intricate system of superhighways links our cities, and jet aircraft whisk us from one end of the country to the other in the time it took our grandfathers to travel to the nearest town. The increased ability to commute longer distances and more leisure time led to a booming travel business and an unbelievable expansion of resort areas along our coasts. I pass no value judgment on whether these changes were desirable or undesirable. I only note that none of them would have taken place without petroleum energy and the internal combustion engine.

The Arab oil embargo and long gasoline lines served as a reminder of the importance of energy. Automobile and airline workers were laid off, and suppliers of these industries were affected by cutbacks in orders. Builders in resort areas suffered nightmares; they were joined by people in the travel business and manufacturers of power boats, snowmobiles, trailers, and other gasoline-consuming pleasure vehicles. We had a brief demonstration of the inescapable fact that lack of energy can lead to economic stagnation, unemployment, and ultimately to spreading poverty and a decline in living standards.

Another beneficial effect of the embargo was to provide an early warning of the consequences of heavy reliance on insecure foreign energy supplies. Reputable estimates by both industry and government experts, prepared in early 1973, indicated that by 1980 we might be dependent on foreign nations for half our oil needs, and that by 1985 this might reach two-thirds of U.S. oil requirements. If we ever come to depend on foreign nations for two-thirds of our petroleum, the measures that have helped us greatly to meet recent energy problems--such as turning back thermostats, driving more slowly, and carpooling--would be exercises in futility. If we are now convinced of the folly of excessive dependence on foreign supplies and of the need to develop our domestic energy resources, the embargo served us well. Had the embargo taken place five years later, when our dependence on Arabian oil was far greater, the result could have been a national disaster instead of merely a painful and unpleasant experience.

In energy presentations, the usual approach is to discuss the shortage, trace its origins, then point the finger of blame at every group except the one you represent.

Today, I propose to eschew Monday-morning quarterbacking. Let us admit that our energy shortfall is the result of many complex forces converging at once: the rising expectations and resulting energy needs of a growing population; restrictions on energy development brought on by an emerging--and too long delayed--concern for man's environment; fragmented and inappropriate decisions by government agencies that discouraged domestic energy development; too much business as usual and lack of foresight by energy industries; and imprudent energy use by American consumers stemming from our long history of energy abundance. We do not have to look very hard to find plenty of blame to pass around.

We are now at the point in the energy crisis where rhetoric must give way to constructive solutions. Let us spend our time addressing the crucial issue of solutions, and leave history to historians.

U.S. energy consumption is massive. It is measured in quadrillions of btu's, billions of tons of coal, trillions of cubic feet of natural gas, or billions of barrels of oil--sums and quantities too big to be grasped. (Speakers should avoid them like the plague.) A few figures, however, are important to keep in mind.

Fossil fuels today provide 95% of U.S. energy. Petroleum accounts for 78% of total energy needs. Oil alone furnishes 45%, which means that the United States consumes about 18 million barrels of oil a day. Coal supplies 17% of our energy, hydropower provides 4%, and nuclear power, the remaining 1%.

Basic logic tells us that there are three ways to solve the energy problem: we must either decrease energy demand, increase energy supply, or do a little of both. Let us take a brief look at the options now open to us.

To cut energy demand, we must do one of two things: (1) restrict demand by allocation and rationing of fuel; (2) reduce demand by encouraging more frugal use of energy by U.S. consumers.

Allocation and rationing are not solutions to energy problems. They will not produce one more barrel of oil, one more cubic foot of natural gas, or one more watt of electricity. They are designed to share scarcity. When shortages reach unacceptable levels, these programs are vital to insure that essential users such as farmers, policemen, and doctors receive adequate fuel, but they never have and never will operate very effectively.

Energy conservation is another matter entirely. It is extremely important. The oil industry and all energy industries are behind conservation programs 100%, and are spending millions of dollars every day on radio, TV, or newspapers to urge conservation. Unlike more permanent solutions, which will take time, we can start practicing energy conservation today. If we can curb demand, supplies will stretch farther.

But energy industries are not seeking permanent 55-mile-per-hour speed limits, permanently chilly homes and offices, poor airplane service, darkened cities, and all the other problems, including higher unemployment. We need to provide citizens with energy, not deny it to them. I can walk ten blocks from my office and find Americans who still have no car, no air conditioner, and no dishwasher. I have seen with my own eyes the poverty in parts of Appalachia. These people have few or none of the energy-using appliances most Americans take for granted. Our country will be in deep trouble if we fail to supply them with energy, and condemn them to a life of poverty.

Energy conservation, of course, involves a lot more than lower speed limits and lower thermostats. As about 40% of energy is used in industry, there is a big potential for energy savings in this field--but it cannot be realized immediately. It requires new equipment and processes to use energy more efficiently and re-use heat. I hope that we will develop a conservation ethic and make wiser use of energy. (I believe we will, especially since energy will be more expensive.) But even if future demand falls short of present forecasts--and these forecasts indicate almost a tripling of energy demand by the end of this century--we must still have huge increases in energy supplies. Energy conservation can reduce the growth rate of demand. The elimination of frivolous energy use is long overdue, but it is only part of the solution to the energy shortfall. We must operate on the supply side of the street as well as on the demand side. How can we increase energy supplies?

For one thing, we can take a fresh look at coal. We have a sufficient supply of coal to last 300 to 500 years, but most of it cannot be used since its high-sulfur content cannot meet environmental regulations. As a result, thousands of manufacturing and commercial firms have been forced to switch from coal to oil--and when these environmental demands could no longer be met, the energy crisis was upon us. The oil industry does not now and never has favored scrapping the Clean Air Act. Protection of the environment is a necessity, not a luxury. Regulations designed to protect human health are essential. A number of regulations in effect, however, are not essential to human health. These can be looked at more critically. There are barriers to increased use of coal, including a lack of readily available coal supplies. There are also, as you well know, problems involved in the mining of coal. I pose as no expert in this field. It is very clear that strip mining cannot and should not be carried out in areas where reclamation is not feasible. It is clear that there are major health and safety problems connected with underground mining. It is also clear that we must solve these problems and make increased use of coal. This is really not an option--it is a necessity. Unfortunately, until coal can be converted to the more environmentally acceptable liquid or gaseous forms, its role in meeting future energy demands will be limited.

The nuclear age is dawning, but very slowly. Almost 30 years after the splitting of the atom, it provides only 1% of our total energy. Nuclear plants have been delayed by both technical and environmental problems. Cumbersome and slow licensing procedures have been a major bottleneck. Fortunately, the government is attempting to speed up and streamline these procedures. The faster they can be brought on-stream the better. However, even if this is done, most experts agree that even by 1985 nuclear power will provide only about 10% of our total energy needs.

Another option is to develop widely-discussed new sources of energy, such as oil and gas from coal, oil from tar sands, nuclear fusion, or solar power. Indeed, although research and development of synthetic and "exotic" fuels must be accelerated, it is essential to look at the time frames for development. Oil shale, coal gasification, and coal liquefaction are mid-term solutions to energy problems. A few synthetic fuel plants may be built starting later in this decade, and many more in the next decade, but they will supply relatively little energy until the end of this century. The use of nuclear fusion and solar power, and harnessing the oceans' tides are solutions to 21st Century energy problems. Although we must have these new technologies available to supplement and eventually replace fossil fuels, to solve today's and tomorrow's energy problems, and those of the next decade, we shall have to rely on existing technology and conventional fuels.

It is clear to anyone who has studied the energy problem that it cannot be solved without oil. What can be done to develop our domestic petroleum resources?

The answere are really not difficult. We have to go where the geologists tell us we can find large amounts of oil and gas, drill for it, construct the necessary pipelines or other transportation facilities needed to move it to refineries, and construct more refineries.

Let's talk first about the Outer Continental Shelf (OCS). While estimates vary, and some new estimates are lower, it is thought to contain about half of our estimated recoverable oil and gas resources. It may contain twice as much of all the oil and gas we have consumed since Colonel Drake struck oil in 1859.

Do not confuse available proven reserves with potentially recoverable reserves. Sometimes, I read articles that leave readers with the impression that we have run out of oil and gas. Nothing could be further from the truth. We are <u>not</u> "out" of oil and gas. We are out of available supplies that we can tap and use <u>now</u>. Oil under the oceans off our coasts or the Arctic tundra cannot heat homes or run cars. We remain rich in energy resources. Certainly our fossil fuels are finite--that is obvious to everyone. Also, we will run low on oil and gas about the middle of the next century and on coal in two or three more centuries, but these resources are available now and we need them _now_.

Why haven't we developed our offshore resources? First, the federal government owns the OCS. Industry must bid for leases if, as, and when the government offers tracts for lease. But lease sales have been small and few. Environmental opposition has strongly influenced government leasing policies, with the Santa Barbara spill in 1969 a powerful factor in curtailing OCS development. Nobody can defend an oil spill, but we think our overall environmental safety record is good. We have worked hard to develop foolproof devices to avoid oil spills, and additional ways to clean up those that do occur. We think the risks of environmental damage from offshore drilling is smaller than the risk of tanker accidents due to collisions, storms, and the like that will occur if we foolishly continue to rely on imports--imports we may or may not receive. Even though only about 2% of the OCS has been explored, we already get close to one-fifth of our domestic oil and gas from it. However, as a result of small lease sales, the percentage actually went down last year for the first time since offshore drilling began a quarter of a century ago. While strict environmental safeguards are essential, and must be rigidly enforced, we must sharply accelerate the development of this rich national resource.

Second, let us talk about Alaska. Six years ago the largest oil field ever discovered in this hemisphere was found at Prudhoe Bay on Alaska's North Slope. This oil is still right there. Although we finally have clearance to build the pipeline after seemingly endless delays, it will be 1977 at the earliest before it is completed and we get the first drop of that ten billion barrels of oil.

Alaska may have a lot more oil, but for six years exploration and drilling have been virtually suspended since there was no assurance that any oil found could be marketed. We really do not know how much oil there is in Alaska. We may find two or three more Prudhoe Bays. We may need a second oil pipeline in Alaska, as well as a gas pipeline. We are confident that this valuable oil and gas can be extracted with minimal impact on the ecology of Alaska.

Although the Outer Continental Shelf and Alaska are believed to contain most of our oil, much is still left in the lower 48 states. The "easy oil" close to the surface has been found, but there is still a lot of it deeper in the ground. The deeper you drill, the more it costs--and costs increase geometrically rather than arithmetically with depth. The production of this oil depends greatly on whether the price of oil is high enough to yield an adequate return on investment. Drilling is a high-risk business. The deepest well ever drilled went down over 30,000 feet in Oklahoma last year--and it was a dry hole. In fact, out of every 100 new-field exploratory wells drilled, only nine strike oil and gas, and only two contain commercially significant amounts. If there is little prospect of an adequate return, the risks will not be taken. An adequate price will also encourage the use of more sophisticated recovery methods, including what is called "secondary" and "tertiary" recovery. This uses water or chemicals to force more oil out of the pores of rocks, where it is tightly held, and bring it to the surface.

As these methods are expensive, their use cannot be justified if oil prices are depressed.

Between 1956 and 1973, the number of wells drilled in the United States fell by more than 50% because of depressed oil prices and the limited access of the industry to the most promising fields. Increased lease sales on the OCS in the past year, the prospect of being able to build the trans-Alaska pipeline, and improved oil prices have finally brought an upturn in drilling. This will not be reflected immediately in terms of increased energy, since it takes three to ten years to develop an oil field--but it is the only route to increased domestic petroleum supplies.

Unfortunately, even if we can increase domestic oil supplies and reduce dependence on foreign nations for crude oil, we have another problem. Crude oil, by itself, is of little value; it must be turned into fuel oil, gasoline, kerosene, and all the other products we need so critically. Even if U.S refineries run flat out, they cannot meet all our needs. There are not enough refineries to do it, because just about every conceivable factor has worked to discourage rather than encourage new refinery construction.

One problem has been uncertainty about crude oil supplies. Obviously, you cannot build a plant without some assurance that the basic raw material needed to operate it can be obtained. Changes in the oil import-quota program last year removed some of this uncertainty, but, obviously, the Arab embargo raised new fears about crude oil availability.

Economics has been another deterrent to new plant construction. A 150,000-barrel-a-day refinery can cost $200 million or more. Before deciding to invest that kind of money, a firm needs some assurance that the expenditure will be recoverable in the marketplace. The situation in the last several years, with Phases I to IV and various off-again, on-again price controls, has not encouraged heavy investment in additional refining capacity.

Another problem involves location or siting. Everyone seems to want refineries as long as they are in someone else's back yard. Environmental opposition has been vocal and effective. One state passed a law completely banning refinery construction in its coastal zone. This problem is especially acute along the East Coast, which has the greatest need for refineries. The Atlantic Seaboard requires 40% of total U.S. oil consumption, but has only 12% of its refining capacity. We need to find reasons to grant permits to build refineries, instead of reasons to block or delay construction.

It is estimated that we will need the equivalent of 60 new refineries to meet expected demands by 1985. Even if this figure turns out to be high, and we need only 40 or 50 as a result of energy conservation or more rapid development of other energy sources, you should know that only one new refinery came on-stream last year, one small one will come on next year, and none the next. This is because only the one refinery is presently under construction--and it takes at least three years to build one. A number of plans were announced last year to build new refineries. The Arab oil embargo shelved some of these plans, but it is hoped that they will now be revived. These announced plans for new refineries have already met powerful opposition. Many are likely to be delayed or never built at all.

We have a few more problems in the oil industry, such as a need for deepwater ports and some worrisome material and manpower shortages. None of these problems is unmanageable if we are determined to remove bottlenecks and produce more oil and gas.

Are we really determined to develop domestic energy resources? Will we be willing to use more coal? Will we speed up development of nuclear power? Will we accelerate development of new fuels? Will we develop our vital oil and gas reserves? Will we continue to practice energy conservation?

Or will we go back to sleep, rely increasingly on foreign energy, and find ourselves one day confronted with far more serious energy problems than we have already experienced?

We cannot be sure. In Congress, we have seen proposals to roll back crude oil prices to levels that would discourage the development of domestic petroleum resources and slow the pace of development of more expensive new fuels. At the very time when the industry requires much capital to undertake drilling and exploration, accelerate research and development, build refineries and deepwater ports, we see proposals to tax away much of the money needed to accomplish these things. There is talk of breaking up or nationalizing the industry. Higher taxes, lower prices, and a less efficient industry are not solutions to energy problems.

We have a chance to reverse our earlier drift toward energy dependence and restore some semblance of self-sufficiency. Can we achieve this by 1980 as President Nixon said last year? I doubt it, but it is the direction that is important and not the timing. Future generations will hold us to blame if, at this key point in our history, we fail to take the steps necessary to insure energy self-sufficiency and enable them to live in a strong, independent, and free nation.

Exhibit C

Heritage of Appalachia
Address by
Cratis D. Williams
Acting Vice Chancellor, Academic Affairs
Appalachian State University
to the
Southern Appalachian Regional Conference
Boone, North Carolina
13 May 1974

Appalachia can be seen as a vanishing frontier and the people as frontiersmen, suspended and isolated, while the rest of the country moves across the twentieth century. Although we are not as far behind now as we were 20 years ago, we are still close enough to the frontier days to describe them with some degree of confidence, for we have become concerned about recording the fullness of our heritage, particularly our cultural heritage.

This cultural heritage probably owes more to the Scotch-Irish than to any other sub-national group. Although we cannot say that a certain percentage of the blood of the average mountaineer is Scotch-Irish, we know it dominates because the Scotch-Irish were a particular kind of people who dominated their communities even when they were outnumbered. I must tell you something about the Scotch-Irish, for this is mainly what we are today in the mountains.

The Scotch-Irish, first of all, were survivors. They were a hardy group who had achieved a homogeneity over a period of 2,000 years by being pushed as remnants before various invaders into the hilly country of the middle of Great Britain--the Scottish border. They were not Scotsmen as we typically think of Scotsmen, nor were they English. They were a strange mixture, not only of the Scots and the English, but of other invaders who in turn were forced into the hills. This meant that they developed a physical quality that differentiated them from other British people. More than anything else, they became the kind of people who could survive on a shoestring. They were resourceful; they knew how to make do; and this in time affected their basic philosophy. They were, therefore, among the first to pitch wholeheartedly into the Reformation as it developed on the island of Great Britain, and their whole philosophy and history prepared them for Calvinistic theology, which they embraced with great fondness. They were, of course, in the center of the War of the Reformation. They followed Cromwell and John Knox. They were troublemakers. They were stubborn. They were literalists.

When the time came to resettle North Ireland, the Crown thought it best not to pick people who would in time either mix with the Irish or feel any sympathy for them. This meant that the Highland Scots were excluded. The English people themselves, being good Episcopalians, were still close to Catholicism. The ideal people to interest in going to Ireland were ones who would have nothing to do with Catholicism, namely, these middle Scotch-Irish who at that time had no label. So North Ireland, after the defection of the Earl of Tyrone, was resettled by these people, where for the first time in their history they had an opportunity to show what they could do. They developed linen industries that were a threat to the London merchants. They knew how to develop the soil to make it productive. They developed the first system of education similar to a public school system in America. They became the best educated common people in Europe.

Within a 100 years, they became a threat to the established order. Laws had to be passed to protect the rest of English civilization against the advances of the Scotch-Irish. Tax laws were passed so that their linen industries could be held in place, and at that point the Scotch-Irish began to hate the British. Then the famines came and, by the middle of the 1730s, the Scotch-Irish had to move out. They came to America.

At this time they found much land already taken in America. They had to pay indentureships because they were very poor. They came as bondsmen and paid off their indentureships often by serving as instructors or tutors in the homes of the wealthy. In time, when land was available along the border, they took it up. Here they reestablished their culture, supported by a hardy outlook on life and sustained by a Calvinistic philosophy that enabled them to be fatalistic about whatever lay ahead. They multiplied rapidly because they believed in large families. They were patriarchal because they thought father was the head of the household. The woman accepted this role and deferred to his wishes, as she still does today.

Along the border they fought back the Indians. They went into the valleys and brought forth whatever was there. They were not yet differentiated from other frontiersmen. (They were not labeled as mountaineers until after the Civil War.) When the Revolution came, however, they remembered their experiences with the British in North Ireland, and almost to a man, were anti-British. When the time came to say "Let us see what we can do with Ferguson at Kings Mountain," they all came together without any rehearsal. They marched on Kings Mountain and took it, though mountain men were not soldiers in the usual sense, and they lacked some of the niceties and points of honor of soldiers. When the British (really, they were not British but sons of South Carolina--Tories, who were nice people then--and who simply wanted to defend the colonies against the intruders) came marching down the hill waving their white flags, the Scotch-Irish accepted them as prisoners of war but, not knowing what to do with them, they lined them up and shot them. There is still a quality of violence about us. (You can forgive me for anything I say, because I am a mountaineer. My people were all on the border at the time of the Revolution, and they have lived there ever since. I have in my background all those mountaineer traits, including whiskey-making and mountain feuds.)

What did the Scotch-Irish bring with them? When they came to the border, they were supra-representative of our settlers. Probably they had higher intelligence than any other one group that came to the borders. They furnished the leadership that went over the mountains and into the valleys, carved out the Northwest Territory, and moved beyond the Mississippi. The cousins stayed in the valleys in the mountains and multiplied--like rabbits--because this is the way mountain people do.

When the Civil War came, they were on the wrong side, and by this mistake, they fated themselves as mountaineers later. There had been no differentiation before the Civil War. That the mountain folk remained loyal to the Union was not known to either the North or the South while the war was going on. After the war was over, it became obvious to those who were in power again in the South that the mountaineers had been traitors. Consequently, such tax resources as were available in the states were not shared with the Appalachian area, but were used to reward the faithful. The road and the school funds were used to help those who had been good. As the mountaineers were allowed to support themselves only on lands that had no tax value, some public schools closed for 18 to 20 years. This meant three or four generations of youngsters who were absolutely illiterate and, though the grandfathers had come to the mountains with calfbound copies of the English poets, the grandsons could not spell their own classical names. They usually gave their children classical names, but these became disordered by the time the illiterate grandsons of the first illiterate generation were ready to write their names again. This also happened to some of the family names. Mountain culture became an oral culture. All that had been known in illiterate fashion settled down to the oral way. There was a redacticism in culture, when the English language itself went backward, and travelers began to observe things that reminded them of Anglo-Saxon. Those who came, looked, and listened said "A-ha! Pure Anglo-Saxon still being spoken." There is some doubt about that, but this purest old-fashioned English is a part of our culture.

There had been great theologians, but now the grandsons were illiterate and their theology was simple folklore--passed on by word of mouth. Even the ministers could not read the Bible, but their theology was sound; if they knew _how_ to preach, they could be ordained because it was assumed they knew _what_ to preach. In the meantime, of course, with the revival along the border, mountain people had learned to compromise their theology so that there could be an "experience" of knowing that one is among the elect. Consequently, mountain people, although they were most theological and religious, waited for an "experience" before becoming a "joiner." They admired the flesh and the devil and found sin so delightful that they postponed the day of salvation as long as possible! The young people then were missed by the church completely, and it became an organization of older people. No matter what the denomination was, the basic theology was still Presbyterian. Forty-seven different brands of Baptists invaded the mountains, but were all basically Presbyterian. The Methodists were very successful in the mountains, but wherever they went, the basic theology remained Presbyterian. Religion was conservative, old-fashioned, and literal. It was a religion of the old people, and one became a "jiner" simply to protect himself from whatever waited after death, for religion had no particular bearing on community life. It was religion, pure and simple, not to be confused with social purpose, interpretation, or even conduct for that matter, because many people were most skillful in using religion as a cloak for their devilment.

The artistic traditions were carried on as "foolishment," if you please. This word "foolish" does not mean foolish in the sense you might think, but rather it means "playful." When the mountain woman says, "Oh, this is just a bit of my foolishment," she means it is creativity in her mode and place. We have in this attitude the whole tradition of mountain crafts in the sense that they are used just as gimcracks. On the other hand, when women were quilting and had time to be playful, they were careful about the patterns they used. If they simply needed bed covering, they made crazy quilts. The men were the same way. If the blacksmith had time to be playful, he turned out something delightful, but most of the time he was doing something practical. He was always modest and apologetic about his artistic creations, his "little bits of foolishness."

One did not <u>learn to play</u> an instrument, but simply <u>played</u> an instrument. This is an aspect of the Calvinistic view of life--you are either predestined to play an instrument or you are not, and if so, you pick it up and play it. If you are not, all the practice in the world could not help. The same thing is true of an ability to sing. This meant, of course, that mountain folk, being conservative people, carried on the old traditions of singing--the chanting of the Middle Ages, the "histing" of tunes, the exclusion of instruments from their religious services, the best singer in the community simply "tuning his nose" in the manner of Chaucerian characters, and everyone else joining in. There was no part-singing and no attempt to be artistic, for such was not religious. (You remember that Plato excluded the poets from his Republic. Poets fool people, and Presbyterian mountain folk had basically the same notion about the arts.) They found art a little sinful. They were always apologetic about art, even though they were quite skillful with it.

Mountaineers were also conservative politically, extremely rugged, and independent, and these qualities we still have. We have a whole tradition of spoken English that is now different from any other part of the English-speaking world, though it is different more in quantity than in quality. We have the singing tradition, wherein people not only know more of the old ballads than anybody else in the English-speaking world, but also being in the tradition, they know how to use it to make ballads of their own. Now the country has been invaded from outside, and the old people who know these things are dying. We are interested in preserving our traditions for contemporary and future generations. Similar communities and groups in the past were allowed to dissipate their traditions without recording them for posterity, but we have the equipment and facilities nowadays to preserve them. As a matter of fact, we have seen in our own generation the rejection of things associated with contemporary civilization for things that have been in the mountains from the beginning. This is the proper use of our traditions. We should like to preserve them for the future.

JUST RELEASED — BOOKS WE ALL HAVE BEEN WAITING FOR
Superb books by, for and about
people of Western North Carolina and the Southern Appalachians

001 "... a right good people"
by HAROLD WARREN
"One of a limited number (of books) that will win the approval of native mountain people."—*Loyal Jones, Director, Appalachian Center, Berea*
128 pages: 37 ills.　　　　paper $2.50

002 Down to Earth—People of Appalachia
by KENNETH MURRAY
"The memory will last forever."—*Ambrose Manning, Professor of English, East Tennessee State University*
128 pages; over 200 ills.　　paper $2.95

003 Bits of Mountain Speech
by PAUL FINK
A bodacious collection of tidbits of mountain speech. "Excellent ..."—*Rogers Whitener, in Folk Ways and Folk Speech*
32 pages　　　　　　　　paper $1.25

004 Western North Carolina Since the Civil War
by DRS. INA and JOHN VAN NOPPEN
"A proud, positive history of a proud and independent people ... Superb ... Should be in every home."—*Dr. W. H. Plemmons, President Emeritus, Appalachian State University*
436 pages; 132 ills.; indexed　cloth $12.95

005 Western North Carolina Since the Civil War
by DRS. INA and JOHN VAN NOPPEN
　　　　　　　　　　　paper $4.95

006 The Birth of Forestry in America
by CARL ALWIN SCHENCK
A reprint of the illustrated history of the first school of forestry in America, which was founded in Western North Carolina at the Biltmore Estate. "It will hold your attention—don't fail to read it."—*Journal of Forestry*
224 pages; illus.　　　　cloth $10.95

007 The Birth of Forestry in America
by CARL ALWIN SCHENCK
　　　　　　　　　　　paper $4.50

008 The Southern Appalachian Heritage
Seventy full four-color illustrations plus a full color cover; 20,000 word text, including ballads, recipes, folklore, history, etc.; shrink wrapped. "Without a doubt the most beautiful, delightful, big book about our colorful region ever produced ... Long overdue."—*Borden Mace, Executive Director, Appalachian Consortium*
　　　　　　　　　　　paper $5.95

009 Toward 1984: The Future of Appalachia
SOUTHERN APPALACHIAN REGIONAL CONFERENCE
144 pages　　　　　　　paper $2.95

Ordering Information:
We offer 10% discounts when three (3) or more books are ordered
Add 3% N. C. sales tax where applicable
We pay postage and handling charges on all prepaid orders

Order from:
The Appalachian Consortium Press
407 East Howard Street
Boone, North Carolina 28607

www.ingramcontent.com/pod-product-compliance
Lightning Source LLC
Chambersburg PA
CBHW070918160426
43193CB00011B/1510